KU-150-141

photography by Ditte Isager

jason
atherton

foreword by Ferran Adrià

# maze
### the cookbook

quadrille

# dedication

To my wife Irha, my daughter Keziah and my parents... I love you all so much. It is your continuous support that makes my career possible.

# foreword

It has been ten years since Jason Atherton spent a season with us at El Bulli. During that time, I caught a glimpse of his potential future as a great chef. Since then, I have followed his journey with interest and I'm delighted to see now that our hopes and his aspirations have been reached. Each season we have around fifty cooks at El Bulli and, after so many years, it is impossible to remember them all. But there is always one chef that stands out from the others, and that was the case with Jason.

He is a magnificent cook that left his mark with us, not only because of his remarkable professionalism, but also because of his personable approach ... one of the values that counts most at El Bulli. During his time with us, Jason was a fundamental element to the team that made that season a success. His work today, together with our friend Gordon Ramsay, has transformed everything he strived for in our restaurant into a brilliant reality of his own.

Now I'm fortunate enough to introduce Jason's first cookbook, which recognises his excellent leading role in the kitchens at London's Maze restaurant. It couldn't have happened any other way. This role reflects Jason's great sensibility and, more importantly, it reveals a new voice in the world of food – a voice that undoubtedly, we will hear more of in the years to come. For readers, this cookbook brings to life the philosophies of Jason's cooking and the seduction of his recipes, and I wish him all the luck he deserves.

**Ferran Adrià**

**Editorial director** Anne Furniss
**Creative director** Helen Lewis
**Project editor** Janet Illsley
**Recipe testing** Emily Quah
**Photographer** Ditte Isager
**Food styling** Jason Atherton and James Durrant
**Props stylist** Lucy Attwater
**Design assistant** Nicola Davidson
**Production** Ruth Deary

First published in 2008 by
Quadrille Publishing Limited
Alhambra House
27–31 Charing Cross Road
London WC2H 0LS
www.quadrille.co.uk

Cataloguing in Publication Data: a catalogue record for this book is available
from the British Library.

ISBN: 978 184400 597 0

Printed in China

# notes

• All spoon measures are level unless otherwise stated:
1 tsp = 5ml spoon; 1 tbsp = 15ml spoon.
• All herbs are fresh and all pepper is freshly ground black pepper unless otherwise suggested.
• Egg sizes are specified where they are critical, otherwise use large organic or free-range eggs.
• If you are pregnant or in a vulnerable health group, avoid those recipes that contain raw egg whites or lightly cooked eggs.
• Oven timings are for fan-assisted ovens. If you are using a conventional oven, increase the temperature by 15°C (1 Gas Mark). Individual ovens can deviate by as much as 10°C from the setting, either way. Get to know your oven and use an oven thermometer to check its accuracy.
• Timings are provided as guidelines, with a description of colour or texture where appropriate, but the reader should rely on their own judgement as to when a dish is properly cooked.

# contents

When I first started cooking at the county hotel in Skegness at the age of sixteen, I didn't have the slightest idea that one day I would be running my own Michelin-starred restaurant. It was a humble beginning. When my family moved to Skegness, we lived in a caravan until my stepfather had earned enough money to house us all. He proved to me what could be achieved through sheer effort. I learnt fast that a recipe of hard work, determination and a little seasoning of good luck will take you a long way in life. When I first became a cook, I decided that if I was going to do this for the rest of my life I'd better be good at it. So I packed my bags and moved to London and, as they say in life, the rest is history.

I've been fortunate to work in some of the world's greatest kitchens and alongside some of the world's finest chefs, but the two chefs I owe most gratitude to are Gordon Ramsay and Ferran Adrià. Gordon's been a constant source of inspiration to me, even before I worked in his kitchens. I still remember my first meal at Aubergine. As I walked away from the restaurant, I knew I had just eaten the food of a modern genius. Few chefs on the planet possess that degree of skill, simplicity and accuracy. I was overwhelmed and didn't think I could possibly achieve those standards with my own food. I've now spent seven years alongside Gordon and, with his continual support, I believe my food is now starting to show some of the same traits. At Maze, we have won lots of awards and a Michelin star, which as a team at the restaurant we are very proud of, but we are even more proud to have a full dining room for lunch and dinner.

As for Ferran Adrià, when I first set foot in his kitchen back in 1997, it was as if someone had picked me up and put me on the moon. All the normal practices of a kitchen were gone. He was making beetroot lollipops to serve as appetisers, vegetable ice creams and sorbets, foams from seawater, desserts with homemade curry powder... Eleven years ago this was outrageous and I hadn't come across anything like it before. I know how Charlie felt when he stepped into Willy Wonka's Chocolate Factory! I realised I was witnessing the start of a food revolution. It was exciting and so inspirational – at last someone was throwing the rule book away and making food fun. After that season with Ferran, I came home to London to embark on my own journey – determined to establish myself as a chef in one of the most fiercely competitive eating capitals of the world.

Having travelled the globe and worked in some of the most respected restaurants in Spain, France, Dubai and Asia, lots of my dishes – like my native lobster Singapore-style – show influences of my travels. It has been a stimulating and challenging jouney, but my biggest challenge to date came when I had the opportunity to open Maze with Gordon. In London the critics are not forgiving, so my head was on the chopping block to make it work! We opened to critical acclaim and have been full ever since, but as a team we know that you are only as good as the last meal you cooked. So here are some of my favourite dishes from our restaurant and also some of my favourite recipes I cook at home. Enjoy...

**JASON ATHERTON**

savoury

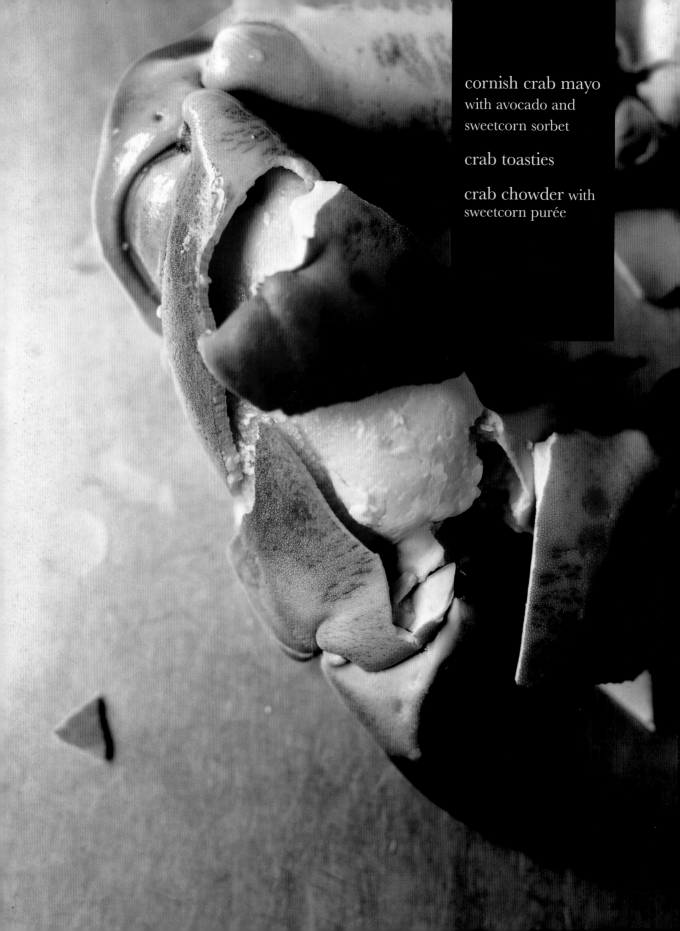

cornish crab mayo
with avocado and
sweetcorn sorbet

crab toasties

crab chowder with
sweetcorn purée

# cornish crab mayo with avocado and sweetcorn sorbet {Serves 6 as a starter}

1 large, freshly cooked crab, about 1.3kg
  (to yield 250g white crabmeat)
100ml mayonnaise (page 246)
juice of ¼ lemon, or to taste
sea salt and black pepper

**AVOCADO PURÉE:**
2 avocados
juice of 1 lime, or to taste
1 tbsp crème fraîche

**TO SERVE:**
sweetcorn sorbet (opposite)  |  chervil sprigs  |  6 tsp oscietra caviar (optional)

To prepare the crab, twist off the claws and legs, then separate the body from the main shell, by prising them apart with a knife and pushing the body upwards until it comes away. Remove the inedible dead man's fingers from the body. Loosen the brown meat in the main shell and spoon into a bowl (use for the crab chowder, page 20, or another dish). Crack the large claws open with a mallet or rolling pin and take out the white meat. Prise out the white meat from the body section and legs, using a fine skewer or crab pick.

Pick over the white crabmeat to check for any small fragments of shell, then tip into a bowl and add the mayonnaise. Mix with a fork, adding the lemon juice and salt and pepper to taste.

For the avocado purée, halve, stone and peel the avocados, then whiz to a purée in a food processor or blender. Add the lime juice and crème fraîche. Whiz to combine and season with salt and pepper to taste.

To serve, spoon the avocado purée into cocktail glasses to half-fill them. Divide the crab mixture between the glasses, forming an even layer, then top with a quenelle of sweetcorn sorbet and a chervil sprig. Finish with a small spoonful of caviar, if you like.

MY FIRST SUMMER *working at El Bulli was one of the most transforming times of my life. I entered a kitchen that had no boundaries and worked on savoury ice creams under chef Ferran Adrià. That's where I drew the inspiration for this sweetcorn sorbet. The caviar is a natural seasoning for the sorbet and the crab mayo is my take on the ubiquitous prawn cocktail. The dish has become a Maze classic.*

# sweetcorn sorbet  {6–8 servings}

340g can sweetcorn kernels in brine
pinch of caster sugar (optional)
sea salt, to taste

Tip the sweetcorn into a food processor or blender, adding the liquid from the can. Whiz until smooth, then pass through a fine sieve into a bowl. Taste and add a pinch of sugar and/or salt if needed.

Churn in an ice-cream machine to a sorbet consistency, according to the manufacturer's instructions. Transfer to a rigid container and put into the freezer (unless serving straightaway). Let the sorbet soften at room temperature for 5–10 minutes before serving.

# sweetcorn purée

I use the same formula (without the freezing) to make a simple purée to accompany several hot dishes, including the crab chowder (page 20). Drain the sweetcorn and warm in a pan with a knob of butter, 3 tbsp reduced chicken stock and 3 tbsp double cream. Whiz and sieve as above, to make a nice thick purée. Check the seasoning and serve piping hot.

# crab toasties {Serves 3–4 as a snack or light lunch}

80–100g white crabmeat
100g cream cheese (at room temperature)
2 tbsp mayonnaise (page 246)
15g dried white breadcrumbs
1 tsp soy sauce
pinch of cayenne pepper
sea salt and black pepper
1 small ciabatta or baguette, thinly sliced on the diagonal

**TO SERVE:**
mesclun and herb salad, dressed with a little vinaigrette

Preheat the oven to 170°C/Gas 3. Pick over the crabmeat and remove any tiny pieces of shell. Soften the cream cheese in a bowl, then mix in the mayonnaise and crabmeat. Add the breadcrumbs and soy sauce, and season with the cayenne and salt and pepper to taste.

Spread the crab mix evenly on the bread slices and place on a baking sheet. Bake in the oven for 10 minutes. Serve with the mesclun and herb salad.

SAVE SOME WHITE MEAT *whenever you prepare a fresh crab to make this tasty snack (or you could use frozen crabmeat). Mesclun is a mixture of young, tender, mild and peppery leaves. Its composition varies, but it usually includes rocket, oak leaf lettuce, lollo rosso, radicchio, frisée, mâche and mizuna. It is available from supermarkets, or better still, assemble your own with leaves from the garden.*

# crab chowder
## with sweetcorn purée {Serves 4 as a starter}

1 onion, peeled
1 large carrot, peeled
1 leek, trimmed
1 celery stick, trimmed
2 tbsp olive oil
4 garlic cloves, peeled
small handful of herb stalks
   (basil, coriander, tarragon)
2 lemongrass stalks
6 white peppercorns
3 star anise

10 coriander seeds
2 tbsp tomato purée
large glass of brandy
large glass of white wine
750ml chicken stock (page 243)
crab shells (optional)
100g brown crabmeat
150ml double cream
50g unsalted butter, in pieces
sea salt and pepper
squeeze of lemon juice, to taste

**TO SERVE:**

sweetcorn purée (page 17) | pinch of paprika | drizzle of olive oil | 4 tbsp white crabmeat

Chop the onion, carrot, leek and celery. Heat the olive oil in a medium pan and fry the chopped vegetables with the garlic until evenly browned. Add the herb stalks, lemongrass, peppercorns, star anise and coriander seeds, then stir in the tomato purée and cook for 3–4 minutes.

Add the brandy and flambé. When the flame dies down, add the wine and let bubble until reduced to a sticky consistency. Pour in the stock (adding any crab shells you may have saved at this stage). Bring to a simmer and cook gently for 20 minutes.

To finish the soup, pass the stock through a fine sieve into a clean pan, pressing the residue in the sieve with the back of a wooden spoon to extract as much flavour as possible. Whisk in the brown crabmeat and the cream and heat through. Reduce slightly if necessary, until you have a good soupy consistency. Whisk in the butter, a little at a time. Finally, season with salt and pepper and add a squeeze of lemon juice to taste. If you wish, froth up the soup with a hand-held stick blender just before serving.

To serve, put a heaped tablespoonful of sweetcorn purée in the bottom of each warm soup bowl and sprinkle with a little paprika and a few drops of olive oil. Add a tablespoonful of white crabmeat to each bowl, pour the hot soup over and serve.

THIS SOUP IS BASED *on a
Maine classic* that's served all
over the east coast of America,
though I have spiced it up a little.
It freezes well – just add the fresh
crabmeat and cream after you
defrost the soup, as you reheat it.

lobster salad
with sweet and sour
dressing, mooli
and ginger salt

native lobster
singapore-style

grilled lobster
with flavoured butter
and herb salad

# lobster salad with sweet and sour dressing, mooli and ginger salt {Serves 4 as a starter}

2 medium uncooked Scottish lobster tails
sea salt and black pepper
¼ large or ½ small mooli (Japanese radish)
olive oil, to glaze

**SWEET AND SOUR DRESSING:**
60ml sherry vinegar
140g thick honey
300ml groundnut oil

**TO SERVE:**
ginger salt (opposite)  |  handful of pickled girolles (opposite)  |  fennel shoots or chervil sprigs

To cook the lobster, bring a pan of salted water to the boil. Uncurl the lobster tails and place them together, head to tail end with their flesh sides touching. Secure with kitchen string. This will ensure that the tails do not curl up during cooking. Add the tails to the pan and poach for 3–4 minutes or until cooked through. Remove from the water and leave to cool slightly. Use a pair of kitchen scissors to snip along the bottom shell of each lobster tail. Prise the shells apart to release the flesh. Wrap the lobster meat in cling film and chill until ready to use.

Peel the mooli and slice lengthways into wafer-thin slices, using a mandolin. Stack the mooli slices and use a small round cutter, 5–6cm in diameter, to stamp out neat discs.

For the dressing, combine the ingredients in a wide bowl and stir until evenly blended. Add the mooli slices one at a time, ensuring that each disc is well coated with dressing before adding another. Cover the bowl with cling film and chill for 30 minutes.

To serve, place 3 marinated mooli discs on each serving plate. Cut the poached lobster tails into bite-sized pieces then rub them with a little olive oil to give them a shiny appearance. Place one or two pieces of lobster on each mooli disc and sprinkle with ginger salt. Cover each one with another mooli disc and sprinkle with a little more ginger salt. Add a few pickled girolles to each plate and garnish with fennel shoots or chervil sprigs. Drizzle the plates with a little sweet and sour dressing and serve immediately.

OUR NATIVE LOBSTERS *are renowned. No matter where in the world I've been working – from France and Spain to Dubai and Asia – I've always found our lobsters are held in high esteem. So, if you can possibly afford to, do use native blues for this dish and the recipes on the following pages.*

## pickled girolles  {Serves 4-6 as a side dish}

200g baby girolles
100ml muscatel vinegar, or cider vinegar
75ml white wine vinegar
100g caster sugar
1 star anise
1 cinnamon stick
3 cloves
1 tsp mustard seeds

Clean the girolles and trim off any rough stems. Place all the remaining ingredients in a pan and stir over a low heat until the sugar has dissolved. Increase the heat and bring to the boil. As soon as the liquid begins to boil, remove the pan from the heat and tip in the mushrooms. Leave to infuse and cool completely. Drain before serving.

The girolles can be kept in the pickling liquor in the fridge for up to a week, but the flavour becomes stronger the longer they are kept. When pairing with the delicate flavour of lobster, they are best served the day you prepare them.

## ginger salt

Simply grind 1 tsp ground ginger and $1\frac{1}{2}$ tsp coarse sea salt together using a pestle and mortar to prepare this seasoning.

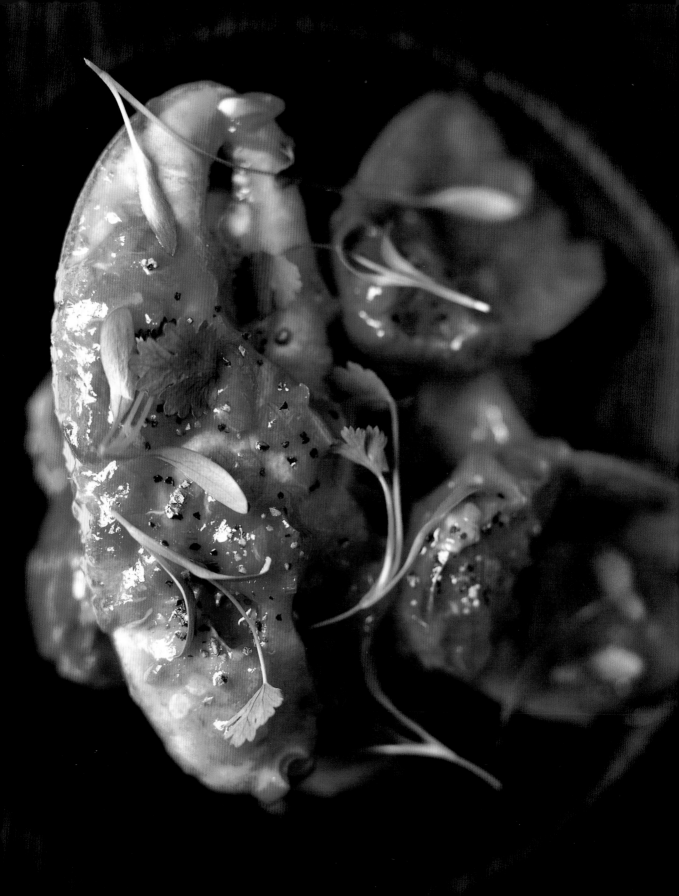

# native lobster singapore-style

{Serves 4 as a main course}

2 large live Scottish lobsters
groundnut oil, for deep-frying
1 onion, peeled and finely chopped
4 garlic cloves, peeled and finely chopped
5cm piece of fresh root ginger, peeled and grated
1 red chilli, deseeded and finely chopped
pinch of fine sea salt
½ tsp ground black pepper
2 tsp black bean paste
4 tbsp sweet chilli sauce

4 tbsp spicy tomato ketchup (page 73)
2 tomatoes, deseeded and diced
1 tbsp sesame oil
1 tbsp soy sauce
1 tbsp caster sugar (optional)
250ml chicken stock (page 243)
1 large egg, lightly beaten
1 tbsp cornflour, mixed with 3 tbsp water
small handful of coriander shoots
    and/or leaves, to garnish

Put the lobsters into the freezer for 2 hours to dull their senses and render them inactive.

To prepare each lobster, hold firmly on a board with the head facing you and point the tip of a heavy chef's knife to the natural cross on the middle of the lobster's head. Firmly and quickly thrust the knife straight through the head until the tip of the knife meets the board, then cut downwards to split the front of the head in two. Turn the lobster around and cut down through the rest of the head and the tail to split the lobster in half.

Twist off the claws and set aside. Remove the dark intestine that runs along the tail and the stomach sac in the head. You can leave in the green liver (known as tomalley) and any greenish black roe or coral (considered to be delicacies). Crack the claws with the back of the knife. Leaving the meat in the shells, chop the tails into smaller pieces.

Heat a 5–6cm depth of groundnut oil in a large wok (or a large, wide pan) until hot. Add the lobster tails and claws and fry for 3 minutes, turning occasionally, until the lobster shells turn red and their flesh is opaque. Transfer to a large bowl and set aside.

Ladle out the excess oil from the wok, leaving about 4 tbsp behind. Add the onion with the garlic, ginger, chilli, salt and pepper and stir-fry for a few minutes until starting to soften. Add the bean paste, chilli sauce, tomato ketchup and tomatoes. Cook for a minute or two, stirring frequently. Tip in the sesame oil, soy sauce and sugar, if using. Mix well, turn down the heat and simmer for a couple of minutes until the tomatoes are soft.

Pour in the stock, then return the lobster pieces to the wok. Increase the heat to high and stir in the beaten egg and cornflour mixture. Cook, stirring continuously, for another 2–3 minutes until the sauce thickens. The dish is now ready to serve.

Transfer the lobster to warm plates, spooning over the sauce. Garnish with coriander and serve. Eat with your fingers... and bread to mop up the delicious sauce.

# grilled lobster with flavoured butter and herb salad {Serves 4 as a main course}

4 live Scottish lobsters
olive oil, to drizzle
black pepper, to grind

**CAFÉ DE PARIS BUTTER:**
250g unsalted butter, softened to room
   temperature
1 tbsp tomato ketchup
1 tsp Dijon mustard
1 tsp capers in brine, rinsed, drained
   and coarsely chopped
30g shallots, finely diced
2 tsp finely chopped curly parsley
2 tsp finely chopped chives
pinch each of dried marjoram and dill

pinch of chopped thyme leaves
½ tsp chopped French tarragon leaves
¼ garlic clove, very finely chopped
2 anchovy fillets, rinsed and finely chopped
1 tsp brandy
1 tsp Madeira
few drops of Worcestershire sauce
pinch of sweet paprika
tiny pinch of mild curry powder
tiny pinch of cayenne pepper
2 white peppercorns, finely ground
1 ½ tbsp lemon juice
pinch of finely grated lemon zest
small pinch of finely grated orange zest

**TO SERVE:**
mixed salad leaves and herbs (frisée, bull's blood, chervil etc) | a little vinaigrette (page 246)

Put the lobsters into the freezer for a couple of hours to subdue them.

To prepare the Café de Paris butter, beat the butter using an electric mixer on low speed until light and creamy. In a separate bowl, thoroughly combine all of the other ingredients, then add to the butter and mix again on low speed until evenly combined.

Place a double layer of cling film, about 20cm in length, on your work surface. Spoon half the butter along the closest edge, leaving 6cm free at both ends. Roll the butter into a log about 5cm in diameter, twisting the ends of the film to seal. Chill for an hour until set.

Preheat the grill to high. Prepare the lobsters and split in two (following the instructions on page 27). Arrange the lobster halves on one large or two smaller baking trays. Drizzle lightly with olive oil and grind over a little pepper. Place under the grill for 3–4 minutes until the flesh turns opaque. Meanwhile, toss the salad in a little vinaigrette.

Place the lobster halves on warm plates and top each with a thick slice of Café de Paris butter. The residual warmth of the lobster will melt the butter. Serve immediately, with a little mixed herb salad on the side.

THE SECRET TO THIS DISH
is the delicious flavoured butter.
It may have a lengthy list of
ingredients but it's easy to make
and you can chill or freeze any
you have leftover to serve with
steak, fish or grilled vegetables.

asparagus with
quail's eggs and pink
grapefruit hollandaise

warm salad of
quail's eggs
and arbroath smokie

roasted asparagus
with a lemongrass,
ginger and tea
vinaigrette

# asparagus with quail's eggs
## and pink grapefruit hollandaise {Serves 4 as a starter}

2 bunches of English asparagus, about 500g
sea salt and black pepper
1 pink grapefruit
3 medium egg yolks
2 tbsp hollandaise reduction (opposite)

250g warm clarified butter (page 242)
pinch of sugar (optional)
8 quail's eggs
few knobs of butter

**TO SERVE:**

pink grapefruit reduction (opposite) | candied grapefruit zest (opposite) | baby chard leaves

For the asparagus, bring a pan of salted water to the boil and have ready a bowl of iced water. Trim the spears and peel the lower part of the stalks. Add the asparagus to the boiling salted water and blanch for 2–3 minutes until just tender. Drain and immediately refresh in the iced water. Drain again and spread out on a clean tea towel.

Next, segment the grapefruit. Cut a slice off the top and bottom of the fruit, then slice off the skin and white pith. Holding the fruit over a sieve set on a bowl, cut out the segments, using a small sharp knife. Squeeze out the excess juice from the membrane, then discard. Chop the grapefruit segments into smaller pieces and set aside.

For the hollandaise sauce, put the egg yolks, 1½ tbsp hollandaise reduction and a pinch of salt into a heatproof glass bowl. Whisk until creamy, then place the bowl over a pan of barely simmering water and beat with a hand-held electric whisk until the mixture forms soft peaks. Slowly pour in the clarified butter, whisking continuously, until the sauce is thick and emulsified. (If the hollandaise becomes too thick, let it down with a little hot water.) Season with salt and pepper, then stir in the diced grapefruit segments. Now taste and adjust the seasoning, adding a little sugar if the hollandaise is too tart. Keep the sauce warm by sitting the bowl in a larger bowl of hot water.

For the quail's eggs, bring a wide pan of water to a simmer; you'll need to poach them in two batches. Crack open the eggs and gently release into the water. Poach for 2 minutes until the whites have set but the yolks are still soft and runny. Remove with a slotted spoon to a plate lined with kitchen paper; keep warm while you cook the second batch. Reheat the asparagus in a pan of simmering water with some butter. Drain well and pat dry.

To serve, drizzle a little grapefruit reduction onto each warm serving plate. Arrange a bundle of asparagus on each plate with the poached quail's eggs. Garnish with candied grapefruit zest and a few baby chard leaves. Serve the hollandaise sauce on the side.

ASPARAGUS IS ONE *of our world-class ingredients that we eagerly await in May. No sooner has it arrived than its short season is over, so we always make the most of it. I learnt this pink grapefruit reduction from Ferran Adrià – it stimulates the tastebuds and enables you to fully appreciate the flavour of the asparagus.*

# pink grapefruit reduction {Makes about 50ml}

100ml freshly squeezed pink grapefruit juice

Pass the grapefruit juice through a fine sieve, pressing the pulp with the back of a spoon, into a pan. Boil until the juice has reduced to a thick, syrupy consistency. Allow to cool, then store in a squeezy bottle until ready to use.

# candied grapefruit zest {Makes about 180g}

2 large grapefruit
200ml grapefruit juice
100g caster sugar

Finely pare the zest from the grapefruit, using a vegetable peeler, then cut off any white pith from it. Slice the zest into very fine strips. Blanch in boiling water for a few seconds, then refresh in cold water. Repeat twice, then drain well. Put the grapefruit juice and sugar in a pan and bring to a simmer. Add the zest strips and simmer very slowly for 1–1¼ hours until the zest is tender and sweet.

# hollandaise reduction {Makes about 50ml}

150ml white wine vinegar
7 white peppercorns
2 tarragon sprigs
2 shallots, peeled and finely diced

Place all the ingredients in a pan, bring to the boil and boil vigorously until the vinegar has reduced by two-thirds. Strain through a fine sieve into a bowl and allow to cool completely. Chill if not using immediately.

# warm salad of quail's eggs
## and arbroath smokie {Serves 4 as a starter or light lunch}

2 Arbroath smokies (smoked haddock fillets)
300ml milk
300ml water
4 quail's eggs

**OYSTER CREAM:**
6 very fresh oysters
100ml double cream
2 tsp Chardonnay or other white wine vinegar

**CONFIT POTATOES:**
500g large Charlotte potatoes, washed
½ garlic bulb, split horizontally
few thyme sprigs
sea salt and black pepper
600ml melted duck fat (or olive oil)
3–4 tbsp mayonnaise (page 246)
handful of chives, snipped
groundnut oil, for deep-frying

**TO SERVE:**
finely sliced shallot rings │ a little vinaigrette (page 246) │ dill sprigs │ olive oil, to drizzle

First, prepare the confit potatoes. Put the potatoes into a pan with the garlic, thyme and a pinch of salt. Pour over the duck fat and lay a piece of crumpled greaseproof paper on top. Cook over a low heat for 30 minutes or until the potatoes are tender when pierced with a skewer. Remove with a slotted spoon and let cool for a minute. Protecting your hands with rubber gloves, peel off the skins while the potatoes are still hot. As you do so, place the skins on a baking sheet in a single layer. Chop the potatoes and place them in a large bowl with the mayonnaise, chives and seasoning. Mix well, then taste and adjust the seasoning.

Preheat the oven to 100°C/Gas ¼. Dry the potato skins in the low oven for 10–15 minutes until crisp. Turn off the oven and leave the potato skins inside to cool slowly.

For the oyster cream, shuck the oysters over a sieve set on a bowl to collect the juices. Put the oyster flesh and juices into a food processor and add the cream, wine vinegar and some seasoning. Blend until smooth then pass through a fine sieve into a small serving jug. Keep chilled until ready to serve. Toss the shallot rings in a little vinaigrette.

Heat a 3–4cm depth of groundnut oil in a small, heavy pan and deep-fry the potato skins in batches until golden brown and crisp. Drain on a tray lined with kitchen paper.

For the smoked fish, bring the milk and water to a simmer in a pan. Poach the fish for 2–3 minutes, then drain and flake, discarding the skin and any bones. Add the quail's eggs to a pan of simmering water and cook for 2½ minutes; drain and refresh under cold water.

Divide the potatoes between serving plates. Top with the shallot rings, flaked haddock and quail's eggs. Garnish with dill and the crispy potato skins. Drizzle with a little olive oil and pour a little oyster cream around each plate. Serve thin slices of toast on the side.

# roasted asparagus
## with a lemongrass, ginger and tea vinaigrette {Serves 4 as a starter}

2 bunches of English asparagus,
  about 500g in total
sea salt and black pepper
8 long bay leaves
8 long thyme sprigs
30g butter, chilled and thinly sliced

**LEMONGRASS, GINGER AND TEA VINAIGRETTE:**
1 lemongrass stalk, trimmed and
  finely chopped
3cm piece of fresh root ginger, peeled
  and grated
1 tbsp lemon verbena tea leaves
finely pared zest of 1 lemon
2 tbsp lemon juice
75ml strong black tea, strained
1 tbsp Chardonnay vinegar, or other
  white wine vinegar
1 tbsp caster sugar
pinch of sea salt
4 tbsp olive oil

For the asparagus, bring a pan of salted water to the boil and have ready a bowl of iced water on the side. Meanwhile, trim the woody bases of the spears and peel the lower ends of the stalks. Add to the boiling salted water and blanch for 2–3 minutes until just tender. Immediately refresh the asparagus in the iced water to stop the cooking process. Drain and pat dry with kitchen paper.

Cut the bay leaves into skinny strips. Use a small sharp knife to make four slits at even intervals along the length of each asparagus spear. Thread the slits with strips of bay leaf and thyme sprigs. Heat the grill to the highest setting.

For the vinaigrette, put all the ingredients into a pan and bring to a simmer, then immediately take off the heat and pour into a small teapot or jug.

Scatter the remaining bay leaf strips on a large baking sheet and place the threaded asparagus spears on top. Sprinkle with salt and pepper. Top with the sliced butter and grill for 5–6 minutes. Transfer to warm serving plates, strain the dressing over the grilled asparagus and serve immediately.

marinated beetroot
with goat's cheese,
chard and beetroot
dressing

whipped goat's
cheese, deep-fried
courgette flowers and
truffle honey

beetroot soup with
crème fraîche and
goat's cheese

# marinated beetroot with goat's cheese, chard and beetroot dressing {Serves 6 as a starter}

3 large beetroot, peeled
25g butter
1 thyme sprig
sea salt and black pepper
200g ewe's milk ricotta, soft goat's
cheese or fresh goat's curd

**MARINADE:**
100ml olive oil
2 tbsp Chardonnay vinegar, or other white
wine vinegar
2 tbsp honey
1 tbsp caster sugar
1 tsp thyme leaves

**DRESSING:**
1 tbsp Cabernet Sauvignon vinegar, or other
red wine vinegar
3 tbsp extra-virgin olive oil
few knobs of butter
1 tbsp of toasted pine nuts, chopped

**TO SERVE:**
handful of baby chard leaves (or micro leaves)

WE USE SAIRASS CHEESE, *a ewe's milk ricotta, at the restaurant but goat's cheese or fresh goat's curd would work equally well for this dish.*

Thinly slice two large beetroot using a mandolin. Stack a few larger slices on top of each other and use a 5cm pastry cutter to stamp out small discs. Repeat until you have 36 neat discs. Save the trimmings and set aside.

For the marinade, mix all the ingredients together in a bowl. Add the beetroot discs to the marinade, one at a time, to ensure that they are all well coated. Cover the bowl with cling film and chill overnight.

Cut the remaining beetroot into tiny batons (or cut them into fine dice), again saving the trimmings. Set aside.

Collect all the beetroot trimmings, place in a pan and pour on enough water to cover. Bring to the boil, then lower the heat and simmer for 20 minutes.

Meanwhile, heat the butter in a pan and add the thyme. Season the beetroot batons with salt and pepper, add to the pan and fry for a few minutes, tossing occasionally until they are tender. Drain off the excess butter and leave to cool on a plate lined with kitchen paper. Chill until ready to serve.

Season the soft cheese with salt and pepper and beat with a fork until smooth. Spoon into a piping bag fitted with a small plain nozzle and set aside.

For the dressing, strain off the juice from the pan of beetroot; discard the trimmings. Return the juice to the pan and boil vigorously until reduced to a thick, syrupy consistency. Cool slightly, then mix with the red wine vinegar and olive oil. Season to taste.

Heat the butter in a frying pan and add the pine nuts. Toss for a few minutes until golden brown, then tip onto a plate lined with kitchen paper and leave to cool. Roughly chop the nuts and add to the beetroot dressing.

To serve, place 3 discs of marinated beetroot on each serving plate. Neatly pipe a mound of goat's cheese on the middle of each beetroot disc. Spoon a few beetroot batons on top of each mound, then cover with another marinated beetroot slice. Spoon over the dressing and garnish with baby salad leaves to serve.

# whipped goat's cheese,
## deep-fried courgette flowers and truffle honey {Serves 4 as a starter}

**WHIPPED GOAT'S CHEESE:**

200g soft goat's cheese
2 tbsp crème fraîche
1 tbsp shallot confit (page 247)
sea salt and black pepper

**DEEP-FRIED COURGETTE FLOWERS:**

12 courgette flowers
1 packet tempura batter
groundnut oil, for deep-frying
fine sea salt, to sprinkle

**TO SERVE:**

few chervil sprigs │ few edible flowers (optional) │ truffle honey (or plain clear honey)

Beat the goat's cheese and crème fraîche together in a bowl until smooth, then stir in the shallot confit. Taste and adjust the seasoning. Using two dessertspoons, shape the goat's cheese mixture into neat quenelles and place two on each individual serving plates. Set aside while you prepare the courgette flowers.

Cut the courgette flowers in half lengthways. Make up the tempura batter according to the instructions on the packet. Heat the groundnut oil in a deep-fat fryer or suitable deep, heavy pan to 190°C. A little batter dropped into the oil should sizzle immediately. In batches, dip the courgette flowers into the tempura batter and then gently lower them into the hot oil. Fry for 1–2 minutes until golden all over, turning the courgette flowers halfway through cooking. Remove with a slotted spoon and place on a tray lined with kitchen paper to drain. While still hot, sprinkle with a little fine sea salt. Repeat with the remaining courgette flowers.

Place a few deep-fried courgette flowers on each plate and garnish with the chervil and edible flowers, if using. Drizzle over a little truffle honey and serve at once.

I LOVE *this simple presentation and combination of flavours. Beetroot can be off-putting for a lot of people but is a great-tasting vegetable, virtually fat-free and full of health benefits. Serve the soup chilled in the summer as a refreshing starter, or hot as a winter warmer.*

# beetroot soup with crème fraîche and goat's cheese {Serves 4 as a starter}

500g beetroot (about 4 large ones)
1½ tbsp olive oil
1 large shallot, peeled and chopped
1 garlic clove, peeled and chopped
30g butter
splash of balsamic vinegar
1 litre chicken stock (page 243)
few thyme sprigs, leaves only
sea salt and black pepper

**TO SERVE:**
100g crème fraîche  |  50g soft goat's cheese  |  olive oil, to drizzle
small herb leaves, such as baby amaranth or purple basil (optional)

Peel and finely chop the beetroot. Heat the olive oil in a medium-large saucepan. Add the shallot and garlic and cook, stirring frequently, over a medium heat for 5–6 minutes until the shallot is soft. Add the butter and allow to melt, then tip in the chopped beetroot. Stir well and cook over a high heat for another 5 minutes. Deglaze the pan with a splash of balsamic vinegar and let it boil dry.

Pour in the chicken stock and add the thyme leaves. Bring to the boil, reduce the heat and simmer for about 40–50 minutes or until the beetroot is very soft.

While still hot, transfer the beetroot to a blender or food processor, using a slotted spoon. Pour in some of the stock and blend until smooth. Pass the mixture through a fine sieve into a clean pan. Stir in more of the stock until you reach the desired consistency. Season generously with salt and pepper to taste. Reheat the soup if serving hot, or if serving cold allow to cool down and then chill for a few hours.

Beat the crème fraîche and goat's cheese together in a bowl until smooth. Pour the soup into individual bowls. Drop a spoonful of the crème fraîche mixture in the middle and grind over some black pepper. Drizzle with a little olive oil and garnish with some baby herbs, if you wish.

jerusalem artichoke
soup with duck
ragoût

jerusalem artichoke
risotto with smoked
haddock

winter duck ragoût

# jerusalem artichoke soup
## with duck ragoût {Serves 6 as a starter}

1.5kg Jerusalem artichokes, scrubbed
500ml milk
500ml double cream
sea salt and black pepper
75g butter, diced
1 tsp truffle oil (optional)

**TO SERVE:**
2 braised duck legs with a little reduced braising liquor (page 52)  |  cep purée (opposite)
cep brioche (page 251), optional  |  cep butter (opposite), optional

Thinly slice the Jerusalem artichokes and place them in a pan with the milk, cream and
some seasoning. Add a little hot water, as necessary, to cover the artichokes. Bring to the
boil, then reduce the heat and partially cover the pan. Simmer for 20–25 minutes until
the artichokes are tender when pierced with the tip of a sharp knife. Drain, reserving the
cooking liquor.

While still hot, put the artichokes into a blender or food processor with a little splash
of the cooking liquor and blend to a smooth purée. Stop the machine once or twice to
scrape down the sides, adding a little more cooking liquor as necessary to get a fine purée.
(At this point, you could take out 5 tbsp of the artichoke purée and reserve it for making
the risotto, on page 51.)

Add some more of the cooking liquor to the blender and blend until smooth.
Continue to add more of the liquor until you achieve the desired soup consistency.
Finally, add the diced butter and blend again until smooth. The butter will melt as soon
as it comes into contact with the hot purée and it will give the soup a rich flavour and
shine. Season well and add a teaspoon of truffle oil, if you wish. Pass the soup through a
fine sieve into a clean pan. Set aside.

Remove the meat from the braised duck legs and shred, then moisten with 1–2 tbsp of
the reduced braising liquor. Gently reheat the artichoke soup. Place a teaspoonful of cep
purée in the bottom of each warm soup bowl, then spoon over a little shredded duck
meat. Pour the hot soup around the meat and, if you wish, serve a warm cep brioche and
some cep butter on the side.

# cep purée   {Makes about 180g}

250g ceps or St. George's mushrooms (or chestnut
    mushrooms if the wild mushrooms are not in season), trimmed
50g lightly salted butter
sea salt and black pepper
little splash of Cabernet Sauvignon vinegar, or other red
    wine vinegar
25ml red wine sauce (page 245), optional
60ml double cream

Finely chop the mushrooms. Melt the butter in a wide frying pan then, as it begins to foam, add the mushrooms with some seasoning. Toss over a high heat for a few minutes until they are golden brown and any liquid released has been cooked off. Deglaze the pan with a little splash of vinegar and let it bubble away until the pan is dry. If you have some available, add a little red wine sauce to provide extra flavour to the mushrooms.

Remove from the heat and tip the mushrooms into a blender or food processor. Pour in the cream and blend for a few minutes to a very fine paste. Taste and adjust the seasoning. For a finer result, push the purée through a sieve. Transfer to a bowl and leave to cool.

# cep butter

Mix some of the cooled cep purée with slightly less than double the amount of softened butter. Form into a log on a double layer of cling film and roll to even out the shape. Wrap and chill until ready to use. The flavoured butter keeps well in the fridge for up to 2 weeks and is delicious sliced and spread on toast or warm brioche slices.

RISOTTO IS A *great dish for the home cook and it is, of course, endlessly versatile. This one is flavoured with Jerusalem artichoke purée and topped with soft-cooked smoked haddock for a touch of luxury. The combination of flavours works brilliantly.*

# jerusalem artichoke risotto
## with smoked haddock {Serves 4-6 as a starter}

4 tbsp olive oil
2 shallots, peeled and finely chopped
sea salt and black pepper
300g risotto rice (carnaroli or arborio)
1 litre chicken stock (page 243) or vegetable stock (page 244)
500ml whole milk
300g lightly cured, naturally smoked haddock
75g Parmesan, freshly grated
2 tbsp mascarpone
5 tbsp Jerusalem artichoke purée (page 48)
75g butter, diced

**TO SERVE:**

freshly shaved Parmesan | shredded parsley | micro leaves (optional)

To make the risotto base, heat the olive oil in a pan. Add the shallots, season and cook, stirring frequently, over a medium heat for 5–6 minutes until soft. Add the rice and cook, stirring, for another minute until it is lightly toasted. Pour in 700ml of the stock and bring to a simmer. Cook for about 8 minutes until the rice has absorbed almost all of the stock. (It should not be cooked through at this point.) Drain the rice and spread out on a lightly oiled baking tray to cool it down quickly. Once cooled, cover with cling film and chill until ready to serve.

Ten minutes before serving, put the milk in a wide pan and bring to a gentle simmer. Add the smoked haddock fillets and poach for 2–3 minutes. Remove from the pan and drain well. Flake the fish into large pieces, discarding the skin and any pin bones. Keep warm.

Put the rice and remaining stock into a pan and bring to a simmer. Cook until the rice is al dente and has absorbed most of the stock. Stir in the Parmesan, mascarpone and Jerusalem artichoke purée. Finally, stir in the butter and season well to taste. The risotto should have a creamy consistency and a glossy shine.

Divide the risotto between warm serving plates and top with the flaked haddock. Scatter over some freshly shaved Parmesan and shredded parsley. Serve immediately, garnished with micro leaves if you like.

# winter duck ragoût {Serves 6 as a main course}

6 duck legs
sea salt and black pepper
1 small onion, peeled and roughly chopped
1 small carrot, peeled and roughly chopped
1 celery stick, trimmed and roughly chopped
2 garlic cloves, peeled
1 thyme sprig
1 rosemary sprig

1 bay leaf
400ml dry red wine
400ml port
splash of Madeira
1.5 litres chicken stock (page 243)
500ml veal stock (page 243), or extra
    chicken stock

**TO SERVE:**
garlic potatoes (page 248)  |  coriander carrots (page 248)

Trim the fat and skins from the sides of the duck legs, then season with salt and pepper. Heat a wide frying pan until hot. In two batches, fry the duck legs for 4–5 minutes, turning until golden brown all over. (You don't need to add oil to the pan.) Remove with a slotted spoon to a plate and set aside. Reserve the fat.

Heat 2 tbsp of the rendered duck fat in a large heavy-based pan or a cast-iron casserole. Add the chopped onion, carrot, celery and garlic and fry over a high heat for 4–6 minutes, stirring frequently, until golden brown. Throw in the herbs and deglaze the pan with the wine, port and Madeira. Bring to the boil and let bubble vigorously until the liquid has reduced and is thick and syrupy. Drain off any fat from the duck legs, then add them to the pan and pour in the stocks. If necessary, add a little boiling water to cover them. Bring to a simmer and cook gently for 2 hours until the duck meat is very tender. Leave the duck legs to cool in the braising stock.

Once cooled, remove the duck legs from the pan and set aside. Strain the braising stock through a fine sieve into a clean pan and boil until reduced to a syrupy glaze. Skim off any fat or scum from the surface and check the seasoning.

When ready to serve, gently reheat the duck legs in the reduced sauce, spooning the sauce over them to glaze, and finish the potatoes and carrots. Serve each duck leg with a portion of garlic potatoes and coriander carrots.

braised shin of veal
with pea risotto

chilled pea soup
with parmesan ice
cream

pea and mint
mushy peas
with sole goujons

# braised shin of veal
## with pea risotto {Serves 4–6 as a main course}

**BRAISED VEAL SHIN:**

1 veal shin, about 1.6kg, boned
   and trimmed
4 garlic cloves, peeled and
   finely crushed
few thyme and rosemary sprigs,
   leaves only, chopped
sea salt and black pepper
2–3 tbsp olive oil
1 carrot, peeled and chopped
2 celery sticks, trimmed and chopped
1 onion, peeled and chopped
1 leek, trimmed and chopped
1 bay leaf
1 tbsp tomato purée

500ml dry white wine
1 litre chicken stock (page 243)
1.2 litres veal stock (page 243)

**PEA RISOTTO:**

300g risotto rice
1 bouquet garni (1 bay leaf, few parsley
   sprigs and thyme stalks, tied together)
750ml chicken stock (page 243)
350ml water
5–6 tbsp pea purée (opposite)
75g Parmesan, freshly grated
2 tbsp mascarpone
75g butter, diced

**TO SERVE:**

blanched peas | blanched broad beans (optional) | handful of micro leaves or mâche
edible flowers (optional)

Open out the boned veal shin on a chopping board and rub all over with the garlic, chopped herbs, salt and pepper. Roll up the shin into a log and secure with kitchen string.

Heat 2 tbsp olive oil in a flameproof casserole or heavy-based pan until hot. Add the veal shin and fry for 2–3 minutes on each side until browned all over. Remove to a plate and set aside. Add a little more oil to the pan if necessary, then add the chopped vegetables and bay leaf. Stir over a medium heat for 4–5 minutes until the vegetables are golden brown. Add the tomato purée and cook, stirring frequently, for a couple of minutes. Deglaze the pan with the white wine and let it reduce down until the pan is quite dry. Return the veal to the pan and pour in the stocks to cover. Put a crumpled piece of greaseproof paper on top and leave to simmer for 2½–3 hours until the veal is tender.

Meanwhile for the risotto, put the rice, bouquet garni, 350ml stock and the water in a saucepan and bring to a simmer. Add a little seasoning and simmer for 7 minutes until the rice has absorbed almost all of the liquid. (It shouldn't be cooked through at this stage.)

Drain off the excess liquid and spread the rice out on a lightly oiled baking tray to cool it down quickly. Cover with cling film and chill until ready to serve.

When the veal is cooked, let it to cool in the braising sauce, then lift out onto a plate. Strain the sauce into a clean pan, pushing down on the vegetables in the sieve to extract all the juices. Boil until reduced by two-thirds to a syrupy sauce. Taste and adjust the seasoning.

Meanwhile, unroll the veal and cut it in half lengthways. Re-roll into two thinner logs and wrap each tightly in a double layer of cling film. Chill until ready to serve.

Just before serving, cut the braised veal shin into individual portions and reheat in a pan with the reduced sauce. Return the blanched risotto rice to a saucepan and add the rest of the stock. Bring to a simmer and cook for 4–5 minutes until the rice has absorbed almost all the stock and is al dente. Stir in the pea purée, Parmesan, mascarpone and finally, the butter. Taste and adjust the seasoning.

Place the braised veal shin portions in warm bowls. Divide the risotto between warm serving bowls and top with the blanched peas, and broad beans if using. Garnish the veal with micro leaves, and edible flowers if you like, then serve.

# pea purée   {Makes about 650g}

100g butter
500g frozen peas
about 400ml chicken stock (page 243)
sea salt and black pepper

Melt the butter in a saucepan and tip in the peas. Pour in just enough stock to cover and bring to the boil. Cook for 2–3 minutes until the peas are just tender but still bright green. Immediately drain, reserving the liquid. Tip the peas into a blender or food processor and add half the reserved liquid. Blend to a fine purée, adding a little more of the reserved liquid as necessary to obtain a thick, smooth consistency. While still hot, pass through a fine sieve into a bowl and season to taste. If not using immediately, set the bowl over another bowl of iced water to cool the purée down quickly, then cover and chill.

I LOVE *this veal and pea risotto dish, because it's packed with flavour. Inspired by simple home-cooked food, it is made to look and taste like refined restaurant food. The pea purée gives the risotto an intense taste and colour, and the match with braised veal is sublime.*

PEA SOUP *has a wonderful fresh taste when it's chilled, which is the only way to serve it as far as I'm concerned. If fresh peas are not in season, use good-quality frozen ones – you'll hardly notice the difference. I've added a Parmesan ice cream for a creamy contrast, but you can serve the soup without if you prefer.*

# chilled pea soup
## with parmesan ice cream  {Serves 4 as a starter}

75g butter
1 onion, peeled and finely sliced
250ml chicken stock (page 243)
250ml whole milk
500g frozen peas, defrosted,
    or 500g pea purée (page 57)
sea salt and black pepper

**PARMESAN ICE CREAM (OPTIONAL):**
500ml double cream
140g piece of Parmesan, finely grated

**TO SERVE:**
4 tsp shallot confit (page 247)  |  1 or 2 handfuls of blanched peas
1–2 spring onions, trimmed and thinly sliced  |  handful of pea shoots (optional)
edible flowers (optional)  |  olive oil, to drizzle  |  polenta tuile squares (page 211), optional

To make the Parmesan ice cream, heat the cream in a pan until almost boiling. Take off the heat and stir in the Parmesan. While still hot, whiz in a blender until the cheese has melted and the mixture is smooth. Pass through a fine sieve into a bowl set over a bowl of iced water. Using a hand-held stick blender or a hand-held electric whisk, mix on low speed. It will thicken as it cools. Keep whisking, increasing the speed slightly until it is a thick custard-like consistency. Pour into a freezerproof container and freeze until firm.

For the soup, melt the butter in a pan and sauté the onion over a medium-low heat for 8–10 minutes until soft and translucent. Pour in the chicken stock and milk and bring to the boil. Tip in the peas and bring back to the boil, then take off the heat. (If using pea purée, add the stock and purée to the pan then add a little milk and bring to the boil.)

Transfer the onion and peas to a blender with half the liquor and blend to a smooth purée, adding a little more stock as necessary. You may need to do this in two batches. (If you've used pea purée, simply whiz until smooth.) Pass through a fine sieve into a bowl set over a larger bowl of iced water. Add little more stock to achieve the desired consistency and adjust the seasoning. Stir occasionally as the soup cools, then cover and chill.

When ready to serve, place 1 tsp shallot confit in the base of each chilled soup bowl. Pour the pea soup over and garnish with the blanched peas and spring onions. Scatter over the pea shoots and edible flowers, if using, then drizzle with a few drops of olive oil. Stamp out little rounds of the Parmesan ice cream if serving, using a 5–6cm cutter. Serve sandwiched between polenta tuiles, alongside the soup.

# pea and mint mushy peas
## with sole goujons  {Serves 4 as a main course}

**MUSHY PEAS:**

350g frozen peas

sea salt and black pepper

few mint sprigs, leaves only

1 tbsp Chardonnay vinegar, or other
   white wine vinegar (optional)

**SOLE GOUJONS:**

600–700g sole fillets (or other white fish
   such as brill or plaice), skinned

4 heaped tbsp plain flour

1 large egg, beaten

60g Japanese Panko breadcrumbs

groundnut oil, for frying

**TO SERVE:**

handful of pea shoots (optional)  |  micro leaves (optional)  |  tartare sauce (page 247)

For the peas, bring a pan of salted water to the boil with the mint leaves added. Tip in the frozen peas and blanch for 2–3 minutes until tender. Drain the peas and mint and transfer them to a blender or food processor, adding the wine vinegar if using. Pulse to a rough purée, adding a little boiling water as necessary to obtain the desired consistency. Season well with salt and pepper to taste, and keep warm.

For the sole goujons, check the fish fillets for pin bones, removing any you find with tweezers. Cut the fillets into 2cm thick strips. Tip the flour into a shallow bowl and season with some salt and pepper. Put the egg into another bowl and scatter the breadcrumbs on a plate. Toss the fish strips in the flour to dust evenly all over, then dip them into the beaten egg and finally coat them with the breadcrumbs.

Heat a 2cm depth of groundnut oil in a deep-sided frying pan until hot. A piece of bread should sizzle immediately when dropped into the oil. Fry the fish in batches for 1–2 minutes on each side until golden. Remove and drain on kitchen paper, then sprinkle with a little more salt.

Divide the goujons and mushy peas between warm serving plates. Garnish the peas with a few pea shoots and micro leaves, if you like. Serve a heaped spoonful of tartare sauce on the side.

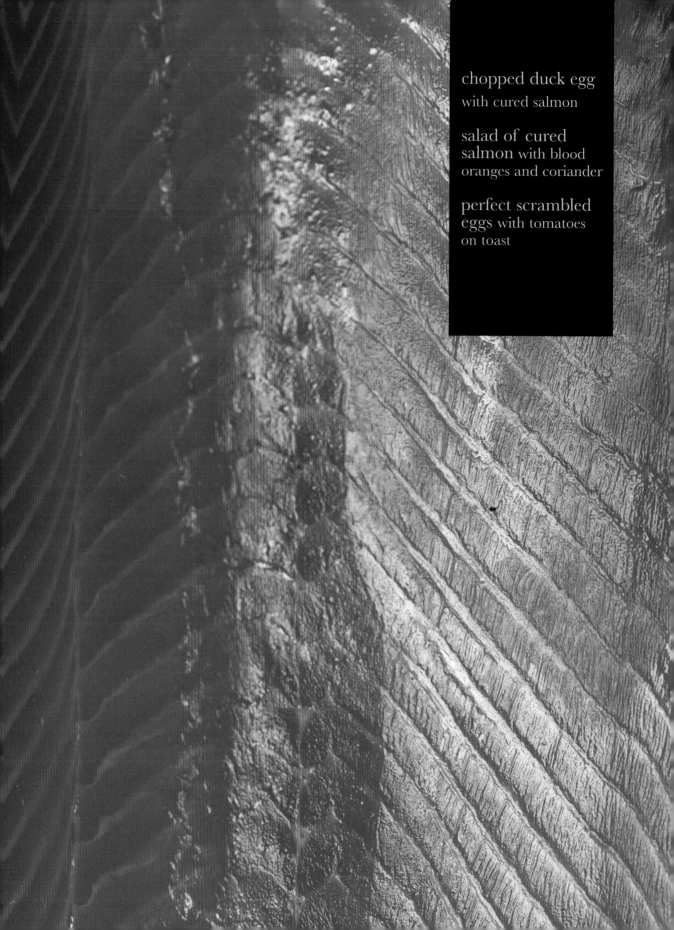

chopped duck egg
with cured salmon

salad of cured
salmon with blood
oranges and coriander

perfect scrambled
eggs with tomatoes
on toast

# chopped duck egg
## with cured salmon {Serves 4 as a starter}

**DUCK EGGS:**

4 duck eggs

sea salt and black pepper

50g unsalted butter, softened

50ml double cream

**SALMON:**

200g lightly cured salmon fillet (from the thick end)

500ml olive oil

**WATERCRESS PURÉE:**

100g watercress

**TO SERVE:**

4 tsp oscietra caviar (optional)  |  few chervil sprigs

SLOW COOKING HAS *become part of the mainstream in most of the best kitchens around the world and it's an advancement I certainly approve of. Slow cooking salmon gives it an incredible, almost butter-like texture, so it really is worth the effort. If you can't get lightly cured salmon, then use fresh fillets instead.*

Bring a pan of water to the boil. Using a slotted spoon, gently lower the duck eggs into the water and simmer gently for 7½–8 minutes. Take out the eggs and refresh in a bowl of cold water, then carefully peel off the shells. The egg whites should be set but the yolks still runny.

Cut each egg in half and scoop out the runny yolks into a large bowl. Chop the egg whites very finely, then add to the egg yolks and mix well. (The eggs can now be chilled if not serving immediately.)

Cut the salmon fillet into 4 portions. Pour the olive oil into a heavy-based pan and place over a very low heat, preferably with a heat diffuser underneath the pan. Heat the oil slowly until it registers 55°C on a cooking thermometer. Add the salmon and poach (or rather confit) at this temperature for 8–10 minutes. You may need to adjust the heat once or twice to the keep the temperature constant.

To make the watercress purée, blanch the watercress in a pan of boiling salted water for about 20 seconds until the leaves are just wilted but still bright green. Drain and blend to a fine purée in a blender or food processor. Transfer to a warm bowl and keep warm.

Reheat the chopped duck eggs in a pan with the butter, cream and seasoning. Stir over a medium-low heat until the eggs are warm but still creamy. Remove from the heat.

Remove the salmon portions from the olive oil using a slotted spoon and pat dry with kitchen paper.

To serve, spoon a little watercress purée onto the base of each warm serving bowl. Cover with the chopped duck eggs, then top with a portion of salmon fillet. Garnish with a spoonful of caviar if you wish, and a few chervil sprigs.

# salad of cured salmon with blood oranges and coriander

400g lightly smoked salmon fillet
   (from the thick end)
750ml olive oil
100g mooli (Japanese radish)
2 blood oranges
½ small fennel
50g red radishes
1 small bunch of coriander

**DRESSING:**
2 tbsp mirin
½ tsp coriander seeds, crushed
2 tbsp caster sugar
4 tbsp olive oil

**TO SERVE:**
small handful of coriander shoots (or coriander leaves)

Cut the salmon into 4 portions. Pour the olive oil into a heavy-based pan and place over a very low heat, ideally using a heat diffuser. Heat the oil slowly until it registers 55°C on a cooking thermometer. Add the salmon and poach at this temperature for 8–10 minutes. You may need to adjust the heat to maintain a constant temperature. Remove the salmon from the oil using a slotted spoon and pat dry with kitchen paper. Cool completely.

Bring a pan of water to the boil and have ready a bowl of iced water. Peel the mooli and thinly slice using a mandolin. Blanch the mooli slices for 1–2 minutes until just wilted, then drain and refresh in the iced water. Drain and pat dry, then place in a large bowl.

Peel the oranges, cutting away all the white pith. Holding the fruit over a sieve set on a bowl to catch the juices, cut out the segments using a small, sharp knife, then squeeze the pith to extract all the juice. Cut the segments into bite-sized pieces and set aside.

Pour the orange juice into a small saucepan and add the ingredients for the dressing. Stir over a medium heat until the sugar has dissolved. Remove from the heat and pour the hot dressing over the mooli slices. Leave to marinate for at least 20 minutes.

Trim off the base of the fennel and slice as thinly as possible. Immerse the slices in a bowl of iced water for a few minutes to crisp them. Do the same with the red radishes, slicing them thinly on the diagonal, then adding them to the iced water.

When ready to serve, drain the fennel and radish slices and place in a large bowl. Remove the mooli slices from the dressing and add to the bowl along with the orange segments. Strain the dressing, add 2–3 tbsp to the salad and toss well.

Divide the salad between individual plates and place the salmon pieces alongside. Drizzle over a little extra dressing and garnish with the coriander to serve.

I DISCOVERED *this technique by mistake! I was parboiling eggs to serve them with runny yolks for a salad, when I realised that chopping up the par-boiled egg and warming it with a splash of cream and butter gave you the perfect scrambled egg!*

# perfect scrambled eggs
## with tomatoes on toast {Serves 4 as a brunch}

**SCRAMBLED EGGS:**

6 duck eggs

75g butter

75ml double cream

sea salt and black pepper

**ROASTED TOMATOES:**

4 ripe plum tomatoes

1 garlic clove, peeled and thinly sliced

1 thyme sprig, leaves only

olive oil, to drizzle

**TO SERVE:**

4 thick slices of Granary bread, toasted | olive oil, to drizzle

First, prepare the roasted tomatoes. Heat the oven to 100°C/Gas ¼. Halve the tomatoes and arrange them, cut side up, on a baking tray. Scatter over the sliced garlic and thyme leaves. Sprinkle with a generous pinch each of salt and pepper and drizzle with olive oil. Roast for 3–3½ hours until the tomatoes are soft.

Now prepare the scrambled eggs, using our unconventional method. Add the duck eggs to a pan of simmering water and cook gently for 7½–8 minutes. Drain and place under cold running water until cool enough to handle, then carefully peel off the shells. The egg whites should be set but the yolks still runny. Cut the eggs in half and scoop out the runny yolks into a large bowl. Chop the egg whites very finely, then add to the egg yolks and mix well. (The eggs can now be chilled if preparing ahead.)

When ready to serve, put the chopped duck eggs in a pan with the butter, cream and seasoning. Stir over a medium-low heat until the egg yolks are scrambled but still creamy. Meanwhile, toast the bread.

Place the hot toast slices on warm serving plates and drizzle over a little olive oil. Arrange the roasted tomato halves on the toast, pile the scrambled eggs on top and serve.

curried monkfish
and celeriac chips
with lime wedges

celery and apple
salad with roquefort
dressing and toasted
walnuts

tempura of
monkfish with apple
and chicory salad and
chilli mango relish

# curried monkfish and celeriac chips with lime wedges {Serves 4 as a main course}

4 chunky portions of monkfish
   fillet, 80–100g each
1 tsp mild curry powder
sea salt
groundnut oil, for frying

**CELERIAC CHIPS:**
1 large celeriac
2 garlic cloves, peeled
few thyme sprigs
generous pinch of sea salt
500ml melted duck fat
groundnut oil, for deep-frying

**TO SERVE:**
dill fronds or coriander sprigs | lime wedges | spicy tomato ketchup (opposite)

First, confit the celeriac for the chips. Cut off the top and base of the celeriac, then slice off the skin following the curve of the root. You want to slice beneath the natural inner circle surrounding the celeriac. Cut the flesh into 1cm thick chips.

Place the celeriac chips in a small pan and add the garlic, thyme and salt. Pour over the melted duck fat to cover and lay a crumpled piece of greaseproof paper on top. Place the pan over a low heat and simmer slowly for 12–15 minutes until the celeriac is tender when pierced with a skewer. Drain the celeriac and lay on a tray lined with kitchen paper to absorb the excess oil. Leave to cool.

When ready to cook, heat the groundnut oil in a deep-fat fryer or other suitable deep, heavy pan to 180°C. A piece of bread dropped into the hot oil should sizzle vigorously. In several batches, deep-fry the celeriac chips for a few minutes until they are evenly golden brown and crisp on the outside. Remove and drain on a tray lined with kitchen paper. Sprinkle with a little salt and keep warm while you cook the fish.

Roll the monkfish fillets in the curry powder mixed with a little salt. Heat a thin film of oil in a frying pan until hot. Add the monkfish portions and fry for 4–5 minutes, turning until golden brown on all sides. Transfer to a warm plate and rest for a couple of minutes.

Arrange the fish and chips on warm serving plates and garnish with dill or coriander. Serve with lime wedges, and a small bowl of ketchup on the side.

THIS IS A WITTY *take on a British classic. I often put it on our lunch menu and it's always popular. The homemade ketchup is delicious and well worth making if you can get really flavourful tomatoes. Try it and you'll probably never reach for that bottle on the supermarket shelf again.*

# spicy tomato ketchup {Makes about 400ml}

500g vine-ripened tomatoes
75g caster sugar
1 tsp white peppercorns
2 tsp sea salt
olive oil, to drizzle
3 garlic cloves, peeled and sliced
small bunch of basil
500ml tomato juice
few dashes of Tabasco sauce
sea salt and black pepper

Preheat the oven to 180°C/Gas 4. Roughly chop the tomatoes and toss them in a large bowl with the sugar, peppercorns, salt and a drizzle of olive oil. Spread the tomatoes out in a casserole dish and drizzle with some more olive oil. Bake for about 1 hour, stirring the mixture once or twice until the tomatoes are soft and slightly caramelised. Add the garlic slices, basil and tomato juice and give the mixture a stir. Return to the oven for another 30 minutes.

Transfer the tomato mixture to a blender or food processor and whiz to a fine purée. Pass through a fine sieve into a saucepan and bring to the boil. Let the mixture bubble until it has thickened and reduced by a third. Add the Tabasco and adjust the seasoning, adding salt and pepper to taste. Allow to cool completely, then transfer to a sterilised jar. Keep chilled and use within a week or two.

# celery and apple salad
## with roquefort dressing and toasted walnuts {Serves 4 as a starter or light lunch}

3 celery sticks, trimmed and peeled
1 baby gem lettuce, outer leaves removed
1 Granny Smith apple
squeeze of lemon juice
1 large chicory bulb, trimmed
50g Roquefort
handful of toasted walnuts

**ROQUEFORT DRESSING:**
100g Roquefort
2–3 tbsp boiling water
100ml mayonnaise (page 246)
sea salt and finely grated white pepper

**TO SERVE:**
deep-fried celery leaves (optional)

First, make the dressing. Crumble the Roquefort into a bowl, then whisk in the boiling water until the mixture is creamy and smooth. Stir in the mayonnaise and season with salt and pepper to taste.

Cut the celery sticks in half lengthways, then cut into 4cm long batons and place in a large bowl. Separate the lettuce leaves and add them to the bowl. Halve and core the apple, then slice thinly. Stack the apple slices and cut into thin matchsticks. Squeeze over a little lemon juice to prevent them from discolouring, then add to the salad. Separate the chicory leaves, add to the salad and toss everything together.

Divide the salad between serving plates and crumble over the Roquefort. Scatter over the toasted walnuts, saving one or two for the dressing. Top with a few deep-fried celery leaves, if you like. Spoon a generous amount of Roquefort dressing onto the side of each plate and finely grate over the reserved walnuts.

I HAVE A DEEP *love of Southeast Asian cuisine and the inspiration for this dressing comes from my wife's home in the Philippines. You might be surprised by the ready-made tempura batter (which you can buy from Asian food stores), but I find it produces a lighter result than homemade batter.*

# tempura of monkfish
## with apple and chicory salad and chilli mango relish {Serves 4 as a light lunch or starter}

600g monkfish fillet, about 150g
  each, trimmed
1 packet tempura batter
groundnut oil, for deep-frying
sea salt and black pepper

**SALAD:**
1 chicory bulb, trimmed
1 Granny Smith apple
squeeze of lemon juice
olive oil, to drizzle

**CHILLI MANGO RELISH:**
1 large ripe, but firm, mango
1 red chilli (or to taste), deseeded and
  finely chopped
1 small red onion, peeled and finely
  chopped
few baby gem lettuce leaves, finely
  shredded

**TO SERVE:**
handful of coriander shoots (or leaves)

First, prepare the relish. Peel the mango and cut the flesh away from the stone. Whiz a quarter of it in a blender or food processor to a fine purée. Cut the rest into 5mm dice and tip into a bowl. Add the chilli, onion and mango purée and toss to mix. Set aside.

For the salad, separate the chicory leaves. Halve and core the apple, then slice thinly. Stack the apple slices and cut into thin matchsticks. Immediately toss the chicory and apple in a bowl with a squeeze of lemon juice, a drizzle of olive oil and some seasoning.

Slice the monkfish thinly on the diagonal and pat dry with kitchen paper. Make the tempura batter, following the packet instructions. Heat the groundnut oil in a deep-fat fryer or other suitable deep, heavy pan to 190°C. The oil is hot enough when a little batter dropped into it sizzles vigorously. You will need to cook the monkfish in several batches. Take a handful and, one at a time, dip each monkfish slice into the batter and lower into the hot oil. Fry for 1 minute until the batter is crisp and golden. Drain on kitchen paper and sprinkle lightly with salt.

Just before serving, stir the shredded lettuce into the relish and spoon into individual serving dishes. Pile the salad onto serving plates and arrange the monkfish tempura alongside. Garnish with coriander and serve at once, with the chilli mango relish.

tuna and mackerel
salad with mooli,
lime, vanilla and
cucumber

tuna tartare with
bloody mary sorbet

marinated
mackerel
with spiced aïoli

# tuna and mackerel salad
## with mooli, lime, vanilla
## and cucumber {Serves 4–6 as a starter}

1 mackerel, about 300g, filleted
  and skinned
600g centre-cut sashimi-grade tuna
  (from the thick end)
¼ mooli (Japanese white radish),
  peeled

**SOY AND LIME DRESSING:**
90ml dark soy sauce
125ml sesame oil
juice of 2 limes
1½ tsp chopped fresh root ginger
1½ tsp chopped garlic

**TO SERVE:**

vanilla and lime pickled cucumber (opposite) | candied lime zest (opposite)
pickled ginger slices (page 250) | cress or micro leaves | edible flowers (optional)

Check the mackerel fillets for pin bones, removing any you find with tweezers. Put the two mackerel fillets together, boned sides touching and in opposite directions (ie head end next to tail end) and place on a double layer of cling film. Wrap tightly in the cling film and roll on the work surface, holding both ends of the cling film, to get a neat log. Freeze for 1–2 hours until just firm. This will make it easier to slice the mackerel thinly.

Cut off any dark bits from the tuna and trim to a neat log, similar in width to the mackerel log. (Save the trimmings for tuna tartare, overleaf). As with the mackerel fillets, roll the tuna log in a double layer of cling film, then freeze for 1–2 hours until just firm.

For the dressing, combine all the ingredients in a small bowl and leave to infuse for 30 minutes. Then pass the dressing through a fine sieve and pour into a squeezy bottle or screw-topped jar.

When ready to serve, unwrap the tuna and mackerel logs and slice as thinly as possible, using a sharp knife. (We use a meat slicer to get wafer-thin slices at the restaurant.) Finely grate the mooli and press into little mounds.

Arrange the tuna and mackerel slices, overlapping, on individual plates. Put two or three mounds of mooli on each plate. Dot the pickled cucumber over the fish, then scatter over the candied lime zest and pickled ginger slices. Shake the dressing well and drizzle generously over the fish. Finally, garnish each plate with cress or micro leaves, and edible flowers if you like. Serve at once.

# vanilla and lime pickled cucumber

{Makes about 250g}

juice of 4 limes
250g caster sugar
2 vanilla pods, split and seeds scraped
1 large cucumber

Put the lime juice, sugar, vanilla seeds and pod into a small saucepan and stir over a low heat to dissolve the sugar. Once dissolved, remove from the heat and leave to cool.

Meanwhile, peel the cucumber and quarter it lengthways. Scoop out the seeds, then chop the cucumber into 1cm cubes. Place in a large bowl and pour over the vanilla and lime marinade. Set aside to infuse for 5–10 minutes. Drain the cucumber before serving.

# candied lime zest  {Makes 250g}

6 limes
180g caster sugar

Bring a small pan of water to the boil. Have a bowl of iced water ready. Finely pare the zest from the limes, using a vegetable peeler. Put the fruit to one side. With a sharp knife, remove any white pith from the zest, then slice into fine matchsticks. Blanch the zest strips in the boiling water for a few seconds, then remove with a slotted spoon and refresh in the iced water. Repeat twice more; drain well.

Halve the limes and squeeze out the juice. Pour into a small pan, add the sugar and stir over a low heat until dissolved. Tip in the blanched lime zest and top up with a little boiling water to cover if necessary. Simmer for 1–1¼ hours or until the zest is tender. You may need to top up with a little hot water occasionally to prevent the syrup from drying out. Allow to cool completely.

Transfer the candied lime zest and syrup to a clean jar, store in the fridge and use within a week or two.

# tuna tartare
## with bloody mary sorbet {Serves 2 as a starter}

200g sashimi-grade tuna
¼ red chilli, deseeded and
    finely chopped
sea salt and black pepper
chilli oil, to drizzle

**BLOODY MARY SORBET:**
1 shallot, peeled and chopped
¼ cucumber, peeled, deseeded
    and chopped
1 small red pepper, deseeded and
    chopped
8 ripe tomatoes
few drops of Tabasco
2 tbsp lemon juice
2 tbsp tomato purée
2 tbsp liquid glucose
20ml vodka

**TO SERVE:**
2 tbsp toasted pine nuts | handful of small mint leaves

First, make the Bloody Mary sorbet. Put the shallot, cucumber and red pepper into a blender or food processor. Halve two of the tomatoes, scoop out the seeds, then chop the flesh. Add to the blender and whiz to a smooth purée. Push through a fine sieve into a bowl and discard the pulp.

Quarter the remaining tomatoes, scoop out and discard the seeds, then tip the tomatoes into the blender. Measure 200ml of the purée and pour into the blender. (Use any leftover for another dish, or to make a Bloody Mary to drink!) Add the Tabasco, lemon juice, tomato purée, liquid glucose, vodka and seasoning to the blender and whiz until smooth. Pass the mixture through a fine sieve into the bowl of an ice-cream machine. Churn until the mixture is almost firm, then transfer to a freezerproof container and freeze until firm.

Chop the tuna fillet into 1.5–2cm cubes and toss them in a bowl with the chopped chilli, some seasoning and a drizzle of chilli oil. Arrange them in individual bowls. Top each tuna cube with a pine nut and a small mint leaf. Drizzle over a little more chilli oil and sprinkle with another pinch of salt. Serve with neat scoops of Bloody Mary sorbet on the side.

THE LAUNCH *of great Japanese restaurants, such as Nobu and Zuma, has inspired confidence in eating raw fish. This dish is nothing more than lightly dressed, fine-quality raw tuna served with an amazing tomato sorbet ... but it is truly superb.*

# marinated mackerel
## with spiced aïoli {Serves 6 as a starter or light lunch}

6 mackerel fillets, with skin
1 small red onion, peeled and
   sliced into rings
small bunch of dill, roughly chopped
2 bay leaves
2cm piece of fresh horseradish, peeled
   and thinly sliced
125ml water
250g caster sugar
250ml white wine vinegar
2 tsp ground allspice
2 tsp yellow mustard seeds
1 tsp caraway seeds
2 tsp each black and white peppercorns

**AÏOLI:**
pinch of saffron
4 garlic cloves, peeled and finely
   crushed
2 medium egg yolks
80g thick creamy mashed potato (optional)
150ml olive oil
sea salt and black pepper

**TO SERVE:**
few saffron strands  |  few handfuls of frisée  |  few chervil sprigs

Check the mackerel fillets for pin bones, removing any with tweezers. If you like, slice off a little skin from the top end of each fillet for an attractive finish. Arrange the fillets skin side down in a fairly deep dish in which they fit snugly, side by side. Scatter the onion, dill, bay leaves and horseradish over the mackerel and chill while you prepare the marinade.

Combine the water, sugar, wine vinegar and spices in a saucepan and stir over a low heat to dissolve the sugar. Bring to the boil, then immediately remove from the heat and leave to cool completely. Pour the cooled marinade over the mackerel, cover the dish with cling film and leave to marinate in the fridge for at least an hour before serving.

For the aïoli, put the saffron, garlic, egg yolks, and potato if using, into a blender or food processor. Blend until the mixture is thick and smooth. With the motor running, slowly trickle in the olive oil until fully incorporated. Season well with salt and pepper.

Drain the mackerel fillets and place, skin side up, on individual plates with some of the marinated onion rings arranged on top. Grind over some black pepper. Spoon a portion of aïoli alongside and sprinkle with a few saffron strands. Garnish the plate with a pile of frisée and a few chervil sprigs. Serve with toasted focaccia or warm baguette slices.

red mullet with
spicy peppers, chorizo
and black olives

spiced fish soup
with tapenade

fried red mullet
wraps with a tomato
and sardine sauce

# red mullet with spicy peppers, chorizo and black olives {Serves 4 as a starter}

4 red mullet fillets, about 100–120g each
2 tbsp olive oil
sea salt and black pepper

**SPICY PEPPERS:**
2 tbsp olive oil
1 red onion, peeled and finely diced
1 fresh chorizo sausage, about 100g, finely diced
1 tsp ras el hanout (Moroccan spice mix)
435g jar sweet roasted peppers
2 tbsp spicy tomato ketchup (page 73)
10 black olives, halved and pitted
few coriander sprigs, leaves only, chopped

**TO SERVE:**
4 tbsp candied aubergine (page 113)  |  few aubergine crisps (page 113)
coriander shoots (or leaves)

WITH ITS MEDITERRANEAN *flavours and colours, this dish has huge appeal. The robustly flavoured pepper stew works best with a strong-tasting fish like red mullet, though sea bass fillets work just as well. Do make the aubergine accompaniments if you have time – they are delicious. Any leftover candied aubergine can be served as a canapé on toast, or with lamb.*

Trim the red mullet fillets to neaten and check them for pin bones, removing any you find with tweezers. Wrap and chill until ready to cook.

For the spicy peppers, heat the olive oil in a frying pan and add the red onion, chorizo and ras el hanout. Fry for 3–4 minutes, stirring frequently. Meanwhile, drain the roasted red peppers, discard any seeds and cut into thin slices. Add them to the pan and cook for another 3 minutes, then stir in the spicy tomato ketchup and olives. Season with salt and pepper to taste. (The peppers can be prepared ahead to this stage and reheated to serve.)

When ready to serve, heat the olive oil in a frying pan until hot. Season the red mullet fillets and fry, skin side down, for 2 minutes until the skin is golden and crisp. Turn over and fry the other side for 30 seconds to 1 minute until the fish is just cooked through. Remove from the heat. Reheat the spicy peppers if necessary and stir through the chopped coriander.

To serve, place a spoonful of candied aubergine in the centre of each warm serving plate or bowl. Top with the red mullet fillets and garnish with the aubergine crisps and coriander. Serve accompanied by the spicy peppers.

# spiced fish soup
## with tapenade {Serves 4 as a starter or light lunch}

3 tbsp olive oil
1 onion, peeled and finely chopped
1 small fennel, trimmed and thinly sliced
2 celery sticks, trimmed and chopped
sea salt and black pepper
200ml dry white wine
500g plum tomatoes, roughly chopped
handful of coriander stalks
pinch of saffron strands
1 star anise

pinch of cayenne pepper
500g red mullet fillets (or trimmings)
600ml water
squeeze of lemon juice, to taste

**PAN-FRIED BABY MULLETS
   AND SCALLOPS:**
4 red mullets, about 100g each
2 tbsp olive oil
knob of butter
4 medium scallops, shelled and cleaned

**TO SERVE:**
fennel purée (page 249), optional
1–2 tbsp tapenade (page 247)

braised baby fennel (page 249), optional
fennel shoots and/or herb leaves

Heat the olive oil in a large saucepan, add the vegetables, season and stir over a high heat for 4–6 minutes until they begin to soften. Add the white wine, stirring to deglaze, and let bubble until the pan is almost dry. Add the tomatoes, coriander stalks, spices and the red mullet. Pour in the water to cover, bring to a simmer and cook gently for 20 minutes.

In two batches, blitz the soup in a blender until well blended, then pass through a coarse sieve into a clean pan. Season to taste with salt, pepper and a squeeze of lemon juice. If you prefer a thicker consistency, boil to reduce and thicken slightly.

When ready to serve, remove any pin bones from the red mullet fillets. Heat 2 tbsp olive oil a frying pan until hot. Season the fish fillets and add them to the pan, skin side down. Fry for 1½–2 minutes until the skin is golden and crisp. Turn over and cook the flesh side for 30 seconds to 1 minute until just firm. Remove and keep warm. Add a knob of butter to the pan. Season the scallops and fry for 1–1½ minutes on each side.

Reheat the soup if necessary and froth up with a hand-held stick blender. Spoon some fennel purée, if serving, into each warm serving bowl. Add a pan-fried scallop and a red mullet fillet, and place a braised baby fennel on the side if serving. Dot with a little tapenade and garnish with fennel shoots and/or herb leaves. Pour the fish soup around the fish and serve straightaway, with some crusty bread.

# fried red mullet wraps with
## a tomato and sardine sauce {Serves 4 as a main course}

1 small loaf of white bread
4 red mullet fillets, about 100–125g
   each, trimmed
2 tbsp olive oil
few knobs of butter

**SAUCE:**

2 tbsp olive oil
1 shallot, peeled and thinly sliced
2 garlic cloves, peeled and chopped
1 thyme sprig, leaves only
sea salt and black pepper
splash of sherry vinegar
4 ripe plum tomatoes, chopped
2 x 120g cans of sardines in tomato sauce
2 tbsp vinaigrette (page 246), optional

**TO SERVE:**

few black olives, halved and pitted | coriander or thyme flowers (optional)

Cut off the crusts from the loaf, then wrap it in a freezer bag and freeze for an hour until firm. Remove and cut the loaf lengthways into thin slices, about 2mm thick. You need 8 good slices. (Use the rest for breadcrumbs.) Let the slices come to room temperature.

Check the red mullet fillets for pin bones, removing any you find with tweezers. Pat the fish dry with kitchen paper. Wrap each fish fillet in a slice of bread, making sure that the overlapping join is on the boned side of the fillet. Lay the wrapped fillets on a plate, each one resting on the overlap, and chill until ready to cook.

To make the sauce, heat the olive oil in a pan and add the shallot, garlic, thyme and a little seasoning. Cook, stirring, for 3–4 minutes until the shallots begin to soften. Deglaze the pan with the sherry vinegar, then add the tomatoes. Cook over a high heat for 4–6 minutes until the mixture has thickened and the pan is quite dry. Add the sardines and break them up with a wooden spoon. Cook for another 2 minutes, to warm through.

Tip into a blender or food processor and whiz to a paste. Push through a coarse sieve into a bowl or pan. For a thicker consistency, boil for a few minutes to reduce. Mix with a little vinaigrette to taste. (The sauce can be served warm or at room temperature.)

When ready to serve, heat the 2 tbsp olive oil in a frying pan until hot. Add the butter, then the red mullet 'wraps' and fry for 2 minutes on each side until the bread coating is golden and crisp. Drain on kitchen paper, then place two wraps on each warm plate and scatter over a few black olives. Garnish with coriander flowers, if you like. Serve a drizzle of the sauce on the side and accompany with a leafy salad.

butter-roasted cod
with silky mash and
spiced lentils

herb-crusted cod
fillets

tomato soup with
cod toasts

# butter-roasted cod with silky mash and spiced lentils {Serves 4 as a main course}

4 cod fillets, about 150g each,
   cut from the thick end
sea salt and black pepper
1 tbsp olive oil
few knobs of butter
few thyme sprigs

**SPICED LENTILS:**
150g Puy or Castelluccio lentils
2 tbsp olive oil
2 shallots, peeled and finely diced
1 fresh chorizo sausage (or 100g
   cured), finely chopped
pinch of smoked paprika
250ml Madeira sauce (page 245)
3–4 tbsp double cream
handful of coriander leaves, chopped

**TO SERVE:**
silky mash (opposite) | olive oil, to drizzle (optional)

First, prepare the spiced lentils. Wash the lentils, put them into a saucepan and add enough water to cover them completely. Bring to the boil, then lower the heat and simmer gently for 30 minutes or until the lentils are tender. Drain well.

Heat the olive oil in a pan and sauté the shallots for 4–5 minutes until they begin to soften. Add the chorizo and paprika and fry for another 1–2 minutes. Pour in the Madeira sauce and cream and let bubble until reduced by a third. Stir in the lentils and warm through. Season with salt and pepper to taste.

When ready to serve, season the cod fillets with salt and pepper. Heat the olive oil and butter in a frying pan until hot, and add the thyme to flavour the oil. Fry the cod fillets, skin side down, for 2–3 minutes, spooning the melted butter over the fish to baste it as it cooks. Turn the fish and cook on the other side for 1–2 minutes, depending on thickness, until it is just cooked through. Remove to a warm plate and rest for a minute while you reheat the silky mash and stir the chopped coriander into the spiced lentils.

Serve the cod on warm plates with generous portions of silky mash and spiced lentils. Drizzle the plates with a little olive oil, if you wish.

COD, LIKE MONKFISH, *is meatier than most other white fish, and pan-roasting it in butter works a treat. However, it is a species on the endangered list, so I only use cod from a sustainable source. The accompanying mash is deliciously rich — you can make it well in advance and reheat it with a splash of milk to serve.*

## silky mash  {4 servings}

750g even-sized La Ratte potatoes, washed
sea salt and black pepper
55ml whole milk
55ml double cream
250g butter

Put the potatoes into a pan of salted water and bring to the boil. Lower the heat and simmer for 20–30 minutes until they are tender when pierced with a small knife. Drain well. Wearing rubber gloves to protect your hands, quickly peel the skins of the potatoes while they are still hot, using a small knife. Mash the potatoes, using a potato ricer if you have one, then push them through a fine sieve to get a really smooth result.

Warm the milk and cream in another saucepan. Put the potatoes back into their pan over a medium-low heat. Add the butter and stir to melt. The mash will become quite greasy at this stage but don't worry. Now stir in the hot milk and cream and you'll find the mash will come together. Season well with salt and pepper to taste and take the pan off the heat. For a silky smooth result, push the mash through a fine sieve once again.

Just before serving, reheat the mash, stirring, over a low heat.

# herb-crusted cod fillets {Serves 4 as a main course}

4 cod fillets, about 140g each
sea salt and black pepper
2 tbsp Dijon mustard
cep butter (page 49), optional
tomato fondue (page 246), optional
olive oil, to drizzle

**SAUTÉED GIROLLES:**
1 tbsp olive oil
25g butter
few thyme sprigs
200g baby girolles, cleaned and trimmed

**TO SERVE (OPTIONAL):**
silky mash (page 97)

**HERB CRUST:**
70g white bread
20g slice of brioche (or extra bread)
large bunch of parsley, leaves only, chopped
handful of thyme, leaves only
80g Gruyère (or Parmesan), freshly grated
150g butter, softened to room temperature

First, make the herb crust. Remove the crusts from the bread and brioche, then tear into pieces. Whiz the bread, brioche, herbs and cheese together in a blender or food processor for a few seconds until the herbs are finely chopped. Add the butter and whiz to a bright green paste. Spoon the mixture onto a large sheet of cling film. Use the cling film to wrap the butter and shape it into a large log, about 5cm in diameter. Holding both ends of the cling film, roll the log on the work surface to even it out. Chill for 1–2 hours until firm.

Preheat the oven to 220°C/Gas 7. Trim the cod fillets and remove the skin and any pin bones with tweezers. Season and place, skinned side up, on a lightly oiled baking tray. Brush the fish with a layer of mustard. If using, thinly slice the cep butter and place on top of the fish, then spread a little tomato fondue over the butter. Cut thin slices from the herb crust and arrange these on top of the fish. (The remaining herb crust can be frozen for later use.) Bake for 4–6 minutes until the fish is opaque and just cooked through.

While the fish is cooking, prepare the sautéed girolles. Heat the olive oil and butter in a wide frying pan until the butter begins to foam. Toss in the thyme and girolles with some seasoning. Cook over a high heat for 3–4 minutes, tossing occasionally. Remove from the heat and keep warm.

Place a herb-crusted fish fillet on each warm serving plate. Divide the sautéed girolles among the plates, drizzle with a little olive oil and serve at once, with silky mash if you like.

# tomato soup with cod toasts {Serves 4 as a starter}

7 vine-ripened plum tomatoes, about 450g
few basil sprigs
3 black peppercorns
250ml tomato juice
sea salt and black pepper
1 red pepper, halved, cored and deseeded
⅓ yellow pepper, deseeded
2 tbsp olive oil, plus extra to drizzle
1 garlic clove, peeled and chopped
1 thyme sprig
1 bay leaf
drizzle of balsamic vinegar, to taste

**GREEN SAUCE:**
3 anchovy fillets in oil, drained
1 garlic clove, peeled
large bunch of flat-leaf parsley, leaves only
1 hard-boiled egg, yolk only
2 tsp white wine vinegar
3 tbsp fresh breadcrumbs
100ml olive oil

**COD TOASTS:**
300ml olive oil, plus 3 tbsp
250g cod fillet, with skin (or trimmings)
½ baguette, thinly sliced
1 garlic clove, peeled and finely crushed

Roughly chop the tomatoes and put into a large bowl with the basil, peppercorns, tomato juice and some salt. Stir well and set aside. Roughly slice the peppers. Heat the olive oil in a pan and sauté the peppers with the garlic, thyme, bay leaf and some seasoning over a medium heat for 6–8 minutes until softened. Discard the herbs, then add the peppers to the tomatoes and stir to mix. Cover the bowl with cling film and chill overnight.

The next day, tip the mixture into a blender and whiz to a purée. Pass through a coarse sieve into a bowl, pressing the pulp to extract all the juices. Taste and adjust the seasoning with some salt and a little drizzle of balsamic vinegar. Chill until ready to serve.

To make the green sauce, put all the ingredients except the olive oil in a food processor. Pulse for a few seconds, then with the motor running, slowly pour in the oil, blending until the sauce emulsifies; do not over-process. Transfer to a screw-topped jar, pour on a thin layer of olive oil, seal and refrigerate. (Save leftover sauce to serve with pasta etc.)

For the cod toasts, heat the 300ml olive oil in a heavy-based pan to a slow simmer. Season the fish and lower into the oil. Poach for 2–3 minutes, then remove with a slotted spoon to a plate lined with kitchen paper to drain. Leave until cool enough to handle, then divide into large flakes, discarding the skin and any pin bones. Season lightly.

When ready to serve, pour the soup into chilled bowls and drizzle over a little olive oil. Lightly toast the baguette slices. Mix 3 tbsp olive oil with the garlic and brush over the toasts. Top with the flaked cod and a little green sauce. Serve warm, with the chilled soup.

loch duart salmon
with baby squid and
crispy chicken skins

salt and pepper
squid

chicken caesar
salad

# loch duart salmon with baby squid and crispy chicken skins {Serves 4 as a starter}

4 Loch Duart salmon fillets, about 100g
  each, skinned
150g baby squid, cleaned and sliced
  into small rings
20g sachet of squid ink (available from
  good fishmongers)
3–4 tbsp olive oil, plus extra to drizzle
sea salt and black pepper

**MINTED PEAS:**
150g fresh or frozen peas
  (defrosted, if frozen)
small bunch of mint
1 tbsp olive oil

**TO SERVE:**

2 tbsp shallot confit (page 247), optional | 2 crispy chicken skins, cut into strips (opposite)
handful of baby sorrel or chard, or micro leaves

Check the salmon fillets for pin bones, removing any you find with tweezers. Cut the baby squid into rings and set aside. For the squid 'paint', mix the squid ink with 1½ tsp olive oil in a bowl and set aside, with a wide paintbrush.

For the minted peas, blanch the peas in a pan of boiling salted water with a few of the mint sprigs added for 2 minutes. Drain, refresh under cold running water and discard the mint. Tip the peas into a small pan (ready for reheating to serve). Remove the stems from the rest of the mint and chop the leaves; put to one side.

Season the salmon on both sides with salt and pepper. Heat a little olive oil in a frying pan until hot. Add the salmon fillets and pan-fry for 1½–2 minutes on each side or until the edges are golden but the fillets are still medium rare in the centre. Remove to a warm plate and leave to rest while you cook the squid.

Add a little more oil to the pan. Season the squid rings and add to the pan. Sauté for 1½–2 minutes or until they turn opaque and are lightly golden around the edges.

In a small pan, warm up the peas, with the shallot confit if using, a little olive oil and some seasoning, then stir through the chopped mint.

To serve, brush four warm serving plates with squid 'paint'. Spoon the minted peas on one side of each plate and place a salmon fillet on top. Scatter some sautéed squid pieces over the squid ink and drizzle the plate with a little olive oil. Garnish with the crispy chicken skins and baby leaves, then serve.

## crispy chicken skins

chicken skins
1 or 2 thyme sprigs
sea salt
drizzle of maple syrup
a little olive oil

Spread the chicken skins on a chopping board and scrape off any excess fat. Put them into a small saucepan with the thyme and some salt and pour on enough cold water to cover. Bring to the boil, then lower the heat to a simmer and cook for 10–15 minutes until tender. Drain well and pat dry with kitchen paper.

Drizzle the cooked chicken skins with a little maple syrup and rub well all over to coat. Spread the skins out on an oiled baking sheet and sandwich with another oiled baking sheet. Weigh down with one or two cans and chill for a few hours or overnight.

Preheat the oven to 170°C/Gas 3. Remove the cans and place the chicken skins, still sandwiched between the two baking sheets, in the oven. Bake for about 15–20 minutes, turning them over halfway through cooking so that they are evenly golden brown and crisp. Remove and cool. Cut into small slices to serve.

# salt and pepper squid {Serves 4 as a starter}

400g baby squid, cleaned
½ packet tempura batter
5 heaped tbsp plain flour
1 tsp fine sea salt
1 tsp freshly ground black pepper
groundnut oil, for deep-frying

**TO SERVE:**

coarse sea salt, to sprinkle | 1 green chilli, finely sliced | 4 lime wedges

Set aside the squid tentacles and slice the body pouches into rings. Pat the squid dry with kitchen paper. Make the tempura batter according to the packet instructions and set aside. Put the flour into a shallow bowl and season with the salt and pepper.

Heat the groundnut oil in a deep-fat fryer or other suitable deep, heavy pan to 180°C. A piece of bread dropped into the hot oil should sizzle vigorously. Dip the squid rings into the seasoned flour to coat all over and shake off the excess. Deep-fry them in batches in the hot oil for 1–1½ minutes until lightly golden and crisp. (Make sure you don't overcrowd the pan or the temperature of the oil will drop.) Drain on kitchen paper and keep warm while you deep-fry the rest of the squid rings.

Now draw the squid tentacles through the tempura batter and deep-fry these until lightly golden and crisp. Drain on kitchen paper.

Sprinkle the deep-fried squid rings and tentacles with a little coarse salt. Divide between warm plates and scatter over the sliced chilli. Serve at once, with lime wedges.

I CANNOT LIVE *with out my squid fix! This is a version of one of the many great dishes at Zuma, a favourite restaurant of mine, so I can't take full credit for it. It is so easy to prepare and makes an ideal canapé to serve with drinks before a dinner party.*

# chicken caesar salad {Serves 4 as a lunch or light main course}

2 chicken breasts, with skin on
500g unsalted butter
4 garlic cloves, peeled
1 thyme sprig
sea salt and black pepper

**SALAD:**
½ small white loaf, crusts removed
8 quail's eggs
8 crispy pancetta slices
2 baby gem lettuce, trimmed
8 freshly marinated anchovies
Parmesan shavings

**DRESSING:**
3 medium egg yolks
4 anchovy fillets in oil, drained
2 small garlic cloves, peeled
  and roughly chopped
2 tbsp white wine vinegar
100g Parmesan, freshly grated
375ml pomace or light olive oil
1–2 tbsp warm water (if required)

First, wrap the loaf of bread for the salad in a freezer bag and freeze for an hour until firm.

Remove the skins from the chicken breasts (save for crispy chicken skins, page 105). Melt the butter in a pan and add the garlic, thyme and seasoning. Turn off the heat and allow to infuse for 30 minutes. Spoon out 3 tbsp of the butter and set aside for the toasts.

Bring the pan of butter to a bare simmer. Add the chicken breasts and poach gently for about 30 minutes until just cooked, turning halfway. Leave to cool in the butter.

Preheat the oven to 130°C/Gas 1. Remove the bread from the freezer and cut into very thin slices. Place them on a baking sheet and drizzle or brush over the reserved butter. Bake for 5–10 minutes until completely dry and crisp.

For the dressing, whiz all the ingredients, except the oil, in a blender or food processor to a smooth paste. With the motor running, slowly blend in the oil until it emulsifies to the consistency of mayonnaise. If the dressing is too thick, let it down with 1–2 tbsp warm water until you obtain the desired consistency. Season well with salt and pepper.

For the salad, gently lower the quail's eggs into a pan of simmering water and cook for 2½ minutes. Refresh under cold running water, then peel off the shells. Fry the pancetta in a dry frying pan until golden and crispy on both sides; drain on kitchen paper.

Separate the lettuce leaves and thinly shred the hearts. Toss them in a large bowl with some of the dressing, then divide between serving bowls. Remove the chicken breasts from the butter and pat dry with kitchen paper. Cut into slices and arrange over the lettuce leaves. Scatter over the anchovies, crispy pancetta, quail's eggs, crispy shards of toast and Parmesan shavings. Drizzle over a little more dressing and serve with a sprinkling of crushed pepper.

steamed smoky sea bass with candied aubergine

papillote of sea bass with provençal vegetables

baba ganoush with hommus and arab bread

# steamed smoky sea bass
## with candied aubergine {Serves 4 as a light main course}

4 fillets of line-caught sea bass, about 100g each
2 tbsp olive oil, plus extra to drizzle
sea salt and black pepper
hickory essence, for brushing
knob of butter
4 baby bok choy, halved lengthways

**SPECIAL EQUIPMENT (OPTIONAL):**
4 cardboard-thin pieces of cedar wood (about 10 x 20cm)

**TO SERVE:**
200g candied aubergine (opposite) | aubergine crisps (opposite)
spicy tomato ketchup (page 73)

Check the sea bass fillets for pin bones, removing any you find with tweezers. Rub a little olive oil over the sea bass fillets, then season well with salt and pepper. If using the cedar wood, brush one side with hickory essence. Bend it over so that the opposite sides meet, to resemble a book, then punch one or two holes along the sides using a paper hole puncher. Place each sea bass fillet on one side of the cedar and fold the cedar around it. Secure the wood by tying two pieces of twine or kitchen string around the punched holes. Repeat for the remaining sea bass fillets. (If you're not using cedar wood, you can simply brush a bamboo steamer with hickory essence, though the steamer will retain a smoky aroma even after washing.) Set aside while you prepare the candied aubergine and aubergine crisps; keep warm.

Bring some water to the boil in a steamer. Slide the sea bass parcels onto the steamer rack (or into the bamboo steamer) and cover with the lid. Steam for 6–8 minutes until the fish is opaque and just cooked through. In the meantime, heat the 2 tbsp olive oil with the butter in a frying pan and sauté the bok choy until tender.

To serve, place a sautéed baby bok choy, a spoonful of candied aubergine and a spoonful of ketchup on each warm serving plate. For an impressive presentation, bring the sea bass parcels to the table and cut the twine to reveal the steamed fillets. Otherwise, transfer the fish fillets to the plates. Serve at once, garnished with the aubergine crisps.

THIS METHOD *of steaming sea bass within thin pieces of cedar wood brushed with hickory essence produces succulent, tender fish with a subtle smoky flavour. Our cedar wood pieces are custom-made but, as an alternative, you could use a bamboo steamer brushed with a little hickory essence (available from specialist suppliers).*

# candied aubergine {Makes about 200g}

500g aubergines (about 1 large or 2 medium ones)
80g caster sugar
2 tbsp lemon juice
1 garlic clove, peeled and finely chopped
handful of thyme, leaves only
60ml hazelnut oil
sea salt and black pepper

Preheat the oven to 200°C/Gas 6 and line a baking tray with a large piece of foil. Cut off the tops and tails of the aubergines, then peel off the skins with a vegetable peeler. Chop the flesh to a fine dice, place in a large bowl and toss with the sugar, lemon juice, chopped garlic and thyme. Spread out on the prepared tray and cover with another piece of foil. Bake for about 45–55 minutes, stirring the aubergines once or twice, until they are very soft and slightly caramelised.

While still hot, transfer the aubergines to a blender or food processor and whiz to a rough paste. With the motor still running, slowly pour in the hazelnut oil and keep blending until the purée is smooth. Transfer the purée to a pan and cook over a high heat to dry it out a little. Season well with salt and pepper to taste.

# aubergine crisps {4 servings}

1 baby aubergine
groundnut oil, for deep-frying
fine sea salt, to sprinkle

Trim the aubergine and slice thinly lengthways, using a mandolin. Heat the groundnut oil in a deep-fat fryer or other suitable deep, heavy pan to 190°C. In batches, deep-fry the aubergine slices in the hot oil until they are golden and crisp. Remove and drain well on a tray lined with kitchen paper. Sprinkle with salt while still warm.

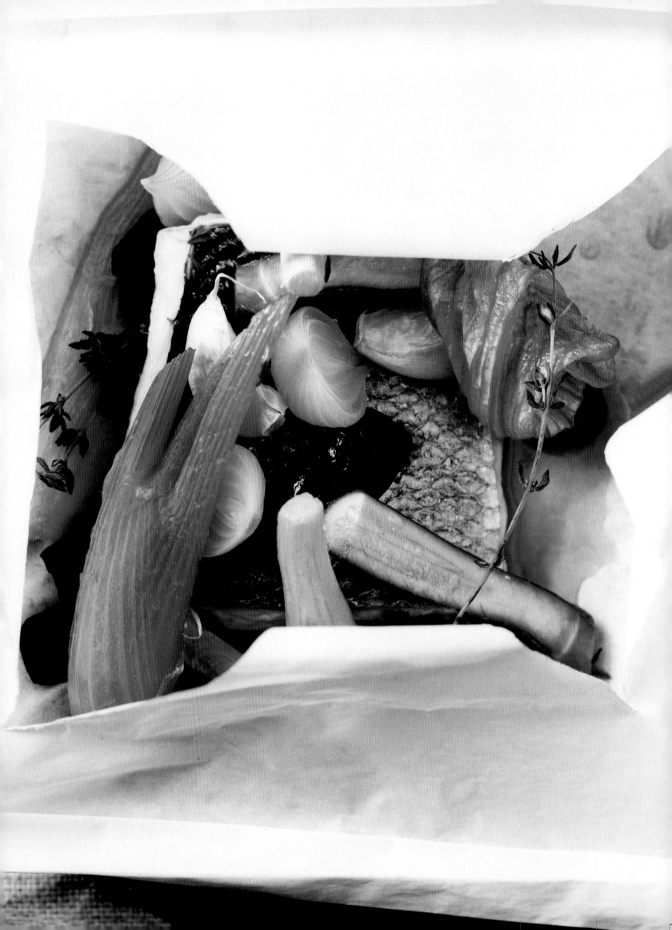

# papillote of sea bass
## with provençal vegetables {Serves 4 as a main course}

4 wild sea bass fillets, about 100g each,
   or 2 small whole fish
1 lemon, halved
2 baby artichokes
sea salt and black pepper
8 baby fennel, trimmed
4 baby courgettes (preferably with
   flowers), trimmed and halved lengthways

8 baby onions or shallots, peeled
12 black olives, halved and pitted
8 garlic confit (page 247)
few thyme sprigs
olive oil, to drizzle
about 200ml fish stock (page 244)

Trim the fish fillets to neaten and remove any pin bones with tweezers. If using whole sea bass, make sure that the fish is cleaned. Chill while you prepare the vegetables.

Squeeze the juice of ½ lemon into a bowl of cold water. To prepare each artichoke, peel away the tough outer leaves with a small sharp knife until you reach the pale green, tender leaves. Trim off the tough skin from the stem and base of the artichoke, then cut vertically into quarters. Immediately drop it into the cold water. Repeat with the rest.

Bring a pan of salted water to the boil with a squeeze of lemon juice added. Blanch the artichokes for 5–7 minutes, depending on size, until just tender when pierced with a skewer. Remove with a slotted spoon and immediately refresh in a bowl of iced water.

Bring the water in the pan to the boil again and blanch the fennel for 2 minutes, then refresh in iced water. Repeat with the courgettes, blanching these for 1 minute. Now blanch the onions for 3–4 minutes. Drain all the vegetables and pat dry with kitchen paper. Halve the onions.

Heat the oven to 200°C/Gas 6. Cut four large baking parchment rectangles, each large enough to wrap a portion of fish and vegetables. Fold them in half to make a crease, then open out. Make the papillotes one at a time. Lay a bass fillet (or whole fish) on one side of the crease. Scatter the vegetables, olives, garlic confit and thyme sprigs around it. Drizzle over the olive oil and sprinkle generously with salt and pepper. Bring the other side of the parchment over the fish and vegetables and fold the edges together firmly to secure the parcel. Just before you completely seal it, add a small squeeze of lemon juice and splash a little fish stock over the fish. Repeat to make the rest of the parcels.

Slide the parcels onto two large baking trays and bake for 8–10 minutes if using fish fillets, about 15 minutes if cooking whole sea bass. Transfer the parcels to individual serving plates and cut them open at the table to release the wonderful aromas.

# baba ganoush with hommus
## and arab bread {Serves 4–6 as a starter or light lunch}

**BABA GANOUSH:**

1½ tbsp olive oil

1 small onion, peeled and finely
   sliced

sea salt and black pepper

½ tsp harissa paste

1 tsp ras el hanout (Moroccan
   spice mix)

1 quantity candied aubergine
   (page 113)

olive oil, to drizzle

1 thyme sprig, leaves only

**HOMMUS:**

400g cooked chickpeas (or a 400g
   can chickpeas, drained)

75ml hot water

125g tahini

75ml extra virgin olive oil, plus extra
   to drizzle

juice of 1 lemon, or to taste

3 garlic cloves, peeled and chopped

1 tsp ground cumin

1 tsp caster sugar (optional)

pinch of paprika

**TO SERVE:**

Arab breads or pittas

To prepare the baba ganoush, heat the olive oil in a pan over a medium heat. Add the onion with some seasoning and cook, stirring occasionally, for 6–8 minutes until soft and golden brown. Stir in the harissa paste and ras el hanout and cook, stirring, for few more minutes to cook the spice. Add the candied aubergine and stir well until heated through. Transfer the mixture to a blender or food processor and whiz for a couple of minutes to a fine paste. Taste and adjust the seasoning with a little more salt and pepper if necessary. Transfer to a serving bowl, cover and set aside.

For the hommus, put the chickpeas, hot water, tahini, olive oil and half the lemon juice into your cleaned blender or food processor. Whiz for a few minutes to a smooth paste, stopping to scrape down the sides once or twice. Add the garlic, cumin and some salt and pepper and blitz again. Taste and adjust the seasoning, adding more lemon juice or a pinch of sugar to balance out the flavours. Spoon into a serving bowl.

Drizzle a thin layer of olive oil over the surface of the baba ganoush and hommus. Sprinkle the baba ganoush with the thyme leaves and the hommus with a little pinch of paprika. Toast the Arab breads or pittas and serve for dipping.

roasted quail with
pear and saffron
chutney

quail skewers
with asian spices

simple foie gras
pâté with pear and
saffron chutney

# roasted quail with pear and saffron chutney {Serves 4 as a starter or light lunch}

2 quails
about 200ml olive oil, plus extra to drizzle
sea salt and black pepper
1 thyme sprig
25g butter
300g foie gras, cut into 1cm slices

**SAUCE:**
2 tbsp olive oil
2 shallots, peeled and sliced

2 garlic cloves, peeled and roughly chopped
1 bay leaf
5 thyme sprigs
¼ tsp black peppercorns
100ml dry white wine
100ml Madeira
20ml honey
20ml soy sauce
150ml chicken stock (page 243)
150ml veal stock (page 243)

**TO SERVE:**
chopped black truffle (optional)  |  few chives  |  pear and saffron chutney (opposite)

Preheat the oven to 220°C/Gas 7. Remove the legs and breasts from the quails and set aside. Remove the giblets from the carcasses and chop up the bones. Put the bones in a roasting tin, drizzle over a little olive oil and roast for 15 minutes until browned.

Season the quail breasts and legs and place in a saucepan with the thyme. Pour over enough olive oil to cover and place over a low heat. Poach slowly for 20 minutes, then remove with a slotted spoon to a plate lined with kitchen paper. Leave to cool.

For the sauce, heat the olive oil in a saucepan and sauté the shallots with the garlic, bay leaf, thyme and peppercorns over medium heat for 5–6 minutes until softened and golden brown. Add the quail bones, then the wine and Madeira. Let bubble until reduced to a sticky glaze. Add the honey and soy sauce and cook for 2–3 minutes. Pour in the stocks and reduce by two-thirds to a syrupy consistency. Strain through a fine sieve into a clean pan.

Fry the quail's legs in a little olive oil, turning until evenly browned. Add to the sauce in the pan and braise over a low heat for 10 minutes until the meat is tender. Keep warm.

Sear the quail's breasts in a little olive oil and butter in a frying pan until golden brown all over. Remove to a plate. Drain excess fat from the pan, then return to the heat. Season the foie gras and pan-fry for 30 seconds on each side until lightly caramelised at the edges.

To serve, drizzle a little sauce over each plate. Place a quail breast on each plate and top with a slice of foie gras. Sprinkle with chopped black truffle if you like, and snipped chives. Spoon a little pear chutney alongside, top with a braised quail leg and serve at once. Borage flowers, if you happen to have some, are a stunning garnish.

# pear and saffron chutney {Makes about 1kg}

160g onions, peeled and diced
200g apples, peeled, cored and diced
200g golden raisins
1 tbsp orange zest
juice of 2 oranges
1 cinnamon stick
1 1/4 tsp ground nutmeg
1/2 tsp cayenne pepper
40g finely chopped fresh root ginger
250ml white wine vinegar
1kg pears, peeled, cored and diced
350g caster sugar
1/4 tsp saffron strands, infused in 1 tbsp warm water

Except for the pears, sugar and saffron, put all the ingredients into a large non-reactive saucepan. Bring to the boil, stirring frequently, and cook until the liquid has reduced by two-thirds. Add the sugar and saffron and cook for another 5 minutes.

Tip in the diced pears and cook gently, uncovered for about 1–2 hours until the chutney is thick and syrupy. The chutney is ready when you can draw a line across the bottom of the pan with a wooden spoon. Spoon into sterilised jars and seal while still hot. Store in a cool place if not serving immediately.

# quail skewers
## with asian spices {Serves 4 as a starter or light lunch}

4 quails
½ tsp Szechuan peppercorns
sea salt
1 tsp five-spice powder

**MARINADE:**
100ml sesame oil
2 tbsp mirin (Japanese rice wine)
2 tbsp soy sauce
1 garlic clove, peeled and
 finely chopped
2cm piece of fresh root ginger,
 peeled and finely chopped
1 red chilli, deseeded and diced

**ASIAN SALAD:**
½ small mooli (Japanese
 white radish)
1 small green mango
handful of coriander shoots or leaves
handful of shiso leaves (or mixed
 baby salad leaves)

First, soak 8 wooden skewers in cold water for at least 20 minutes. Cut along both sides of the backbone of each quail with poultry shears to remove it. Take out the giblets, then rinse the quails and pat dry with kitchen paper. Open out a quail on a chopping board and press down with the palm of your hand to flatten it slightly. Use poultry shears to cut the quail in two so that each half has a breast connected to a leg. Push a skewer through each half, piercing through the leg and breast. Repeat for the remaining quails.

Mix together all the ingredients for the marinade. Set aside half for the salad and brush or rub the remainder over the quails. Lightly toast the Szechuan peppercorns in a dry frying pan until fragrant. Tip into a mortar with a pinch of salt and grind with a pestle until finely crushed. Mix with the five-spice powder and rub over the quails. Cover loosely and leave the quails to marinate in the fridge for 2–3 hours.

For the salad, peel and slice the mooli and mango into thin matchsticks. Put them into a bowl along with the coriander and salad leaves. Toss to mix.

Preheat the grill to the highest setting. Arrange the marinated quails in a single layer on a baking tray. Place under the grill for 10 minutes, turning over halfway, until the skins are golden brown and the meat is firm and cooked through. Leave to rest for a few minutes while you toss the salad with the remaining marinade. Divide the salad between individual serving bowls and serve two quail skewers per person.

# simple foie gras pâté with pear and saffron chutney

{Serves 4 as a starter or light lunch}

500g very fresh chicken or duck livers
300ml milk
25g butter
2 shallots, peeled and finely sliced
1 garlic clove, peeled and finely chopped
1 thyme sprig
350ml ruby port
350g foie gras, cut into 1cm thick slices
sea salt and black pepper

**TO SERVE:**

toasted slices of brioche or country bread | pear and saffron chutney (page 121)

Cut off any discoloured or bloody parts from the livers, then soak the livers in the milk for 1–2 hours. Tip them into a sieve to drain and pat dry with kitchen paper.

Melt the butter in a small pan and add the shallots, garlic and thyme. Cook, stirring occasionally, for 5–6 minutes until the shallots are soft and golden brown. Pour in the port and bring to the boil. Let it boil until reduced down to a syrupy consistency.

While the port is reducing, sauté the foie gras slices in a hot, dry frying pan until golden brown and slightly caramelised. This will only take about 30 seconds on each side. Remove to a colander set over a bowl and set aside.

Pour off the excess oil from the pan and return to the heat. Season the chicken or duck livers with salt and pepper and add them to the pan. Fry for about 5 minutes, turning them over halfway, until the livers well browned, but still pink in the middle. Tip into the colander to join the foie gras.

Remove the thyme from the port mixture. Tip the livers and foie gras into a food processor and add the reduced port with the shallots and garlic. Season well. While still hot, blend to a smooth paste. Taste and adjust the seasoning.

Spoon the pâté into four ramekins and immediately cover each one with cling film. Leave to cool completely, then chill until ready to serve. Serve with slices of toasted brioche and pear and saffron chutney on the side.

THIS PÂTÉ *is very quick and easy, but it won't keep for longer than a couple of days in the fridge. Serve it with the chutney and a simple leafy salad for a perfect lunch.*

slow-cooked chicken
with smoked mussel
and brown bread sauce

lemon and garlic
roasted chicken
with moroccan spices

coq au vin

# slow-cooked chicken with smoked mussel and brown bread sauce {Serves 4 as a main course}

2 Label Anglais chickens, about 1.8kg each
sea salt and black pepper
1kg butter (or 1 litre olive oil)
small bunch of thyme
1 garlic bulb, halved horizontally

**BABY VEGETABLES:**
8 baby turnips
8 baby leeks
8 baby carrots
splash of chicken stock (page 243)
30g butter, diced

**BROWN BREAD SAUCE:**
1½ tbsp olive oil
2 shallots, peeled and finely chopped
100ml dry white wine
500ml chicken stock (page 243)
1 slice of brown bread, crusts
 removed and torn
125ml double cream
2 smoked mussels

**TO SERVE:**
tarragon emulsion (opposite) | few watercress sprigs | crispy chicken skins (page 105)

Remove the legs and wings from the chickens, leaving you with the chicken crowns. Save the wings for the sauce and use the legs for another dish (such as coq au vin, page 132). Rub the chicken crowns all over with salt and pepper.

Melt the butter in a large heavy-based pan and add the thyme and garlic. Lower the heat to just below simmering. The butter should barely move. Add the chicken crowns and lay a piece of crumpled greaseproof paper on the surface of the butter. Poach gently for about 30–40 minutes until the chickens are firm and just cooked through. Remove and leave to cool slightly, then take off the skins and reserve for the crispy chicken skins. Carve out the chicken breasts and return them to the warm butter to keep them moist.

To make the sauce, heat the olive oil in a large saucepan. Add the chicken wings and fry for 3–4 minutes until golden brown all over. Remove and set aside. Add the shallots to the pan and fry, stirring, for 4–6 minutes until soft and golden brown. Deglaze the pan with the white wine and let it bubble until reduced by half. Pour in the chicken stock and return the chicken wings to the pan. Bring to a simmer and cook for 35–40 minutes until the liquor has reduced by two-thirds.

Meanwhile, blanch the baby vegetables in boiling salted water for 3–4 minutes each until just tender when pierced with a skewer. Refresh in a bowl of iced water, then drain.

To finish the sauce, whiz the bread in a blender or food processor to fine crumbs. Strain the sauce through a fine sieve into the blender and add the cream and smoked mussels. Season well with salt and pepper and blitz for a few minutes.

When ready to serve, remove the chickens from the warm butter. Heat the baby vegetables through in a pan with the stock and butter. Gently reheat the brown bread sauce and froth it up using a hand-held stick blender.

Place a chicken breast on each warm serving plate with a little tarragon emulsion. Halve the baby vegetables and divide between the plates. Garnish with watercress sprigs and crispy chicken skins, then pour over the brown bread sauce and serve.

## tarragon emulsion {Makes about 140g}

1 large bunch of tarragon, roughly chopped
1 slice of white toast, crusts removed and roughly torn
1 tsp cider vinegar
1 shallot, peeled and finely chopped
½ peeled garlic clove
50ml olive oil
sea salt and black pepper

Put the tarragon, bread, cider vinegar, shallot and garlic into a blender or food processor and whiz to a fine purée. With the motor still running, trickle in the olive oil; the mixture will emulsify and become smooth. Season well with salt and pepper to taste. If not serving immediately, pour into a clean jar and cover with a thin layer of olive oil. Seal and store in the fridge; use within a few days.

GORDON INTRODUCED *me to Label Anglais chickens a little while ago and I was impressed by their superior flavour and texture. The smoked mussel and brown bread sauce may sound a weird addition, but when you taste it you'll appreciate how well it works.*

# lemon and garlic roasted chicken with moroccan spices

{Serves 4 as a main course}

1 Label Anglais chicken, about 1.8kg

1 tbsp harissa paste

1 tsp ras el hanout (Moroccan spice mix)

2 tbsp olive oil

30g unsalted butter

2 cinnamon sticks

1 thyme sprig

**LEMON STOCK SYRUP:**

5 lemons, quartered

juice of 2 large lemons

1kg caster sugar

sea salt and black pepper

2 litres water

few thyme sprigs

few rosemary sprigs

1 bay leaf

1 head of garlic, halved horizontally

Joint the chicken into 8 pieces and set aside. Put all the ingredients for the lemon stock syrup into a large saucepan and bring to the boil, then lower the heat to a gentle simmer. Add the chicken pieces, except the breasts, making sure that they are covered by the stock syrup. Poach for 10 minutes, then add the chicken breasts and top up with a little hot water if necessary. Gently poach for another 12–15 minutes, depending on the thickness of the chicken pieces. Leave to cool in the hot stock.

Preheat the oven to 200°C/Gas 6. Remove the cooled chicken pieces from the lemon stock with a slotted spoon and pat them dry with kitchen paper. (The strained stock can be used once more but it does become quite bitter with time.) Spread the harissa paste evenly over the chicken pieces then sprinkle over the ras el hanout and some seasoning.

Heat the olive oil and butter in a large ovenproof pan over a medium heat. Add the cinnamon sticks, thyme and 3–4 lemon halves from the stock syrup. Fry for a few minutes until the lemons are slightly caramelised around the edges and the cinnamon and thyme have infused the butter with a lovely aroma. Add the chicken pieces and fry for 4–5 minutes until golden brown. Transfer the pan to the oven and roast for 5 minutes until the chicken pieces are just firm and cooked through. Leave to rest for a few minutes before serving, with new potatoes and green beans or courgettes.

# coq au vin

{Serves 6 as a main course}

6 chicken legs

200g Alsace bacon trimmings, diced

6 shallots, peeled and roughly chopped

1 large carrot, peeled and roughly chopped

1 leek, trimmed and roughly chopped

750ml bottle of red wine

3–4 tbsp olive oil

sea salt and black pepper

1 head of garlic, halved horizontally

few thyme sprigs

1 bay leaf

½ tsp white peppercorns

75ml brandy

75ml port

splash of sherry vinegar

500ml chicken stock (page 243)

500ml veal stock (page 243)

**TO SERVE:**

100g lardons | braised baby onions (page 249) | tarragon emulsion (page 129), optional
few thyme sprigs | wafer-thin slices of toasted white bread (optional)

Put the chicken legs, bacon and vegetables into a large bowl and pour over the red wine. Cover and leave to marinate in the fridge overnight.

Strain off the wine and reserve it for later use. Set the vegetables and bacon aside. Pat the chicken pieces dry with kitchen paper. Heat the olive oil in large cast-iron casserole. Season the chicken legs with salt and pepper and fry for 2–3 minutes on each side until browned. Remove from the casserole and set aside.

Add a little more oil to the casserole, if necessary, then add the vegetables and bacon. Sweat for 8–10 minutes over a medium heat, stirring occasionally, until the vegetables are soft. Add the garlic, thyme, bay leaf and peppercorns and fry for a couple more minutes.

Deglaze the casserole with the brandy, port and sherry vinegar. Let bubble until reduced to a sticky glaze. Pour in the stocks and reserved wine and return the chicken legs. Simmer for 30 minutes until the chicken legs are tender and cooked through, skimming off any scum that rises to the surface from time to time.

Remove the legs to a plate and strain the stock through a fine sieve into a clean, wide pan. Boil it vigorously until reduced to a rich and syrupy sauce. Meanwhile, sauté the lardons in a dry frying pan until crisp.

When ready to serve, return the chicken legs to the reduced sauce and add the braised baby onions and sautéed lardons. Warm through, then divide the chicken and vegetables between warm serving plates. Add a spoonful of tarragon emulsion if serving. Garnish with the thyme sprigs, and white toast if you like. Serve accompanied by vegetables of your choice.

THIS IS *a great way to use up chicken legs, or simply to make a cheap dinner. The tarragon emulsion goes well, but it is not essential. Serve with a mixed salad in the summer, or roasted potatoes and braised cabbage in the winter.*

rack and braised
shoulder of lamb
ras el hanout

warm couscous
salad with lamb
and ras el hanout

braised shoulder
of lamb hotpot

# rack and braised shoulder of lamb ras el hanout {Serves 4 as a main course}

**RACK OF LAMB:**

1 large rack of lamb

sea salt and black pepper

1½ tbsp olive oil

25g butter

**SHOULDER OF LAMB:**

4 large chunks of braised
   lamb shoulder (page 141)

**SPICED ONION AND OLIVE SAUCE:**

2 tbsp olive oil

10 baby onions, peeled and thinly sliced

12 black olives, pitted and thinly sliced

2 tbsp sherry vinegar

½ tsp ras el hanout (Moroccan spice mix)

4 tsp harissa paste

few coriander stalks

few parsley stalks

1 rounded tbsp honey

250ml liquor from the braised lamb shoulder

**TO SERVE:**

white onion purée (opposite)  |  deep-fried onion rings (page 149)

braised baby onions (page 249)  |  confit baby leeks (opposite)

First, prepare the sauce. Heat the olive oil in a saucepan until hot and add the onions with some seasoning. Cook over a medium-low heat, stirring frequently, for 6–8 minutes until they are soft. Tip in the olives and sherry vinegar and increase the heat slightly. Let bubble until the pan is quite dry. Stir in the ras el hanout and harissa paste and cook for another 2 minutes. Add the herb stalks, honey and lamb braising liquor. Give the mixture a stir and boil for 10 minutes. Taste and adjust the seasoning. Discard the herb stalks.

To cook the rack of lamb, preheat the oven to 200°C/Gas 6. Heat the olive oil in an ovenproof pan until hot. Season the rack and fry skin side down for 2 minutes until browned. Turn and sear the other side for 2 minutes. Add the butter and, as it melts and foams, spoon it over the lamb. Turn the lamb around, so that the skin is facing upwards and put the pan into the oven. Roast for 15–20 minutes, depending on the thickness of the rack. The meat should be slightly springy when pressed and a skewer inserted into the thickest part should feel just warm, indicating it is cooked medium rare. Cover with foil and rest for 5 minutes while you reheat the lamb shoulder, sauce and accompaniments.

To plate, carve the lamb rack into portions and rest each piece on a chunk of braised lamb shoulder. (Save extra lamb chops to serve with couscous, page 139.) Place a spoonful of onion purée on the side and top with a few crispy onion rings. Put a couple of braised baby onions alongside, add a confit baby leek and spoon over the sauce. Serve at once.

HERE I'VE COOKED *the main ingredient using two different cooking techniques, so you have a lovely roasted rack of lamb with an intensely flavoured braised shoulder. We serve the dish with four onion dishes, each with a different texture, but you could just make the onion purée and serve some spinach as an accompaniment.*

# white onion purée {4 servings}

1 tbsp olive oil
2 large onions, about 500g, peeled and chopped
sea salt and black pepper
1 thyme sprig
300ml double cream

Heat the olive oil in a saucepan and add the onions with some seasoning and the thyme. Cook gently, stirring occasionally, for 6–8 minutes until they are beginning to soften. Pour in the cream and bring to a simmer. Cook for another 30 minutes until the onions are really soft. Discard the thyme sprig. Drain the onions, reserving the cream, and put them into a blender or food processor with 1 tbsp of the reserved cream. Whiz to a fine purée, then pass through a sieve into a small pan. Return to the heat and cook until the purée is thickened and reduced by two-thirds. Taste and adjust the seasoning.

# confit baby leeks {4 servings}

8 baby leeks, trimmed
sea salt and black pepper
200ml melted duck or goose fat

Put the leeks in a small saucepan with a little seasoning. Cover with melted duck fat and place the pan over a very low heat. Slowly cook for 8–10 minutes until the leeks are tender when pierced with a skewer. Remove and drain well before serving.

THIS IS MY *take on the classic Moroccan lamb tagine. When I lived in Dubai, I was astounded by the wonderful array of fresh spices in the souks and introduced many of them into my cooking.*

# warm couscous salad
## with lamb and ras el hanout {Serves 3-4 as a main course}

2 tbsp sultanas
200g couscous
1 tsp rock salt, crushed
2 tsp ras el hanout (Moroccan spice mix)
3 tsp olive oil
400ml boiling water
1 Granny Smith apple
4 tsp lemon juice, plus a squeeze
1 tsp finely grated lemon zest
4 tsp finely chopped coriander
2 tsp finely chopped rosemary
4 tsp vinaigrette (page 246)

**TO SERVE:**
½ roasted rack of lamb with spiced onion and olive sauce (page 136)

Put the sultanas into a small bowl, pour on a little boiling water to cover and leave to soak for 10 minutes until softened and plumped up. Drain well and pat dry with kitchen paper.

Put the couscous, rock salt, ras el hanout and olive oil in a large bowl and pour over the 400ml boiling water. Give the mixture a quick stir, then cover with cling film and leave to soak for 15–20 minutes.

Meanwhile, peel, core and finely dice the apple, then squeeze over a little lemon juice to prevent it from discolouring. Fork through the couscous to separate the grains and break up any large lumps. Add the apples together with the rest of the ingredients and fork through to mix. Taste and adjust the seasoning.

Warm up the lamb rack and sauce. If necessary, reheat the bowl of couscous, covered with pierced cling film, briefly in the microwave. Spoon the couscous into warm shallow serving bowls. Carve the rack into individual chops and place on top of the couscous. Drizzle over the sauce and serve immediately.

# braised shoulder of lamb hotpot {Serves 4 as a main course}

**BRAISED SHOULDER OF LAMB:**

1 shoulder of lamb, about 2kg, boned
2–3 tbsp olive oil
sea salt and black pepper
1 onion, peeled and cut into 1cm dice
2 celery sticks, trimmed and cut into 1cm dice
2 carrots, peeled and cut into 1cm dice
1 leek, trimmed and chopped
1 garlic bulb, halved horizontally
pinch of rock salt
1 bay leaf

few thyme sprigs
few rosemary sprigs
1 tbsp tomato purée
750ml bottle of white wine
¼ tsp white peppercorns
600ml chicken stock (page 243)
600ml veal stock (page 243)

**TOPPING:**

2–3 large waxy potatoes
25g clarified butter (page 242)

Trim the lamb of excess fat, then cut into chunks. Heat the olive oil in large flameproof casserole. Season the lamb with salt and pepper and fry in several batches for about 2 minutes on each side until evenly browned. Remove to a plate with a slotted spoon.

Add a little more little oil to the casserole and sauté the vegetables with the garlic, salt and herbs over a high heat for 3–4 minutes. Stir in the tomato purée. Cook for 2 minutes until the vegetables are golden brown, then pour in the wine, stirring to deglaze. Bring to the boil and let bubble until reduced to a sticky glaze. Add the peppercorns and pour in the stocks. Return the lamb to the casserole and stir. Partially cover and simmer very gently for 2–2½ hours until the lamb is very tender. Leave it to cool in the braising liquor.

Cook the potatoes in salted water for 15–20 minutes until just tender when pierced with a skewer. Drain and while still hot, peel off the skins. Cut the potatoes into thin slices and spread out on a baking sheet lined with kitchen paper to cool and dry out a little.

Drain the lamb and vegetables in a colander set over a clean pan to save the liquor. (If you're planning to make the recipe on page 136, set aside 4 large chunks of meat and measure out 250ml of the liquor, then boil the rest of it for the hotpot until reduced by one-third.) If using the full quantity of liquor, then reduce by half. Season well to taste.

Preheat the oven to 220°C/Gas 7. Put the lamb and vegetables into a casserole or divide among individual ovenproof dishes. Pour over enough reduced liquor to come just below the lamb and vegetables. Arrange the potatoes slices overlapping on top and brush generously with clarified butter. Sprinkle with salt and place the dishes on a large baking tray. Bake for 15–20 minutes or until the potatoes are golden brown around the edges.

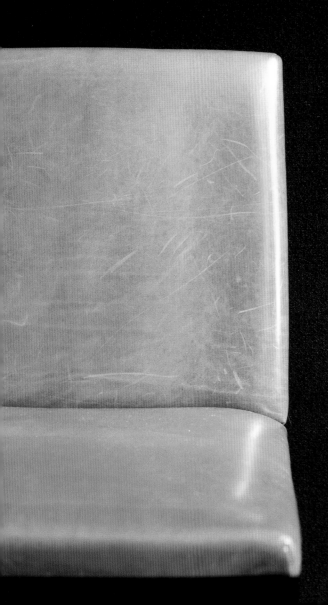

braised ox 'tongue
in cheek'
with ginger carrots

salad of ox tongue
with gremolata
and pecorino

braised ox cheeks
in red wine with
mash and bacon

# braised ox 'tongue in cheek'
## with ginger carrots {Serves 6-8 as a main course}

**BRAISED OX CHEEKS:**

4 ox cheeks

1 large onion, peeled and chopped

2 carrots, peeled and chopped

2 celery sticks, trimmed and chopped

few thyme and rosemary sprigs

1 bay leaf

300ml port

600ml red wine

sea salt and black pepper

2–3 tbsp olive oil

500ml veal stock (page 243)

500ml chicken stock (page 243)

6 black peppercorns

**POACHED OX TONGUE:**

1 ox tongue

1 onion, peeled and sliced

1 carrot, peeled and sliced

1 celery stick, trimmed and sliced

1 litre chicken stock (page 243) or water

50g butter

**TO SERVE:**

horseradish pommes purée (page 161)   |   ginger carrots (opposite)   |   caper raisin purée (opposite)

Trim the ox cheeks of fat and sinew, then put into a large bowl with the vegetables and herbs. Pour over the port and wine. Cover and leave to marinate in the fridge overnight.

The next day, strain off the wine and reserve. Pat the ox cheeks dry with kitchen paper, then season with salt and pepper. Heat 1–2 tbsp olive oil in a sauté pan and fry the cheeks for 2 minutes on each side until browned. Remove to a plate and set aside. Add a little more oil to the pan, tip in the vegetables with the herbs and stir over a medium heat for 4–6 minutes until golden brown. Add the reserved wine, stirring to deglaze, and let bubble until reduced to a syrupy glaze. Pour in the stocks, add the peppercorns and return the ox cheeks to the pan. Lay a crumpled piece of greaseproof paper on the surface. Bring to a slow simmer and cook for 3–3½ hours until tender, stirring occasionally. Leave the ox cheeks to cool in the braising liquor.

Meanwhile, poach the ox tongue. Put it into a saucepan with the vegetables and chicken stock. Top up with water to cover and bring to a low simmer. Partially cover the pan and cook for 2–2½ hours until tender. Top up with hot water as necessary to keep the tongue submerged.

Remove the tongue from the poaching liquid and while still hot, cut or peel off the skin and gristle with a small, sharp knife. Leave to cool completely, then cut 6–8 thin slices. (Save the remainder to use for sandwiches or to make the salad on page 146.)

When the ox cheeks have cooled, remove them from the pan and set aside. Pass the braising liquor through a muslin-lined sieve into a clean pan. Boil until reduced to a thick and syrupy sauce. Season with salt and pepper to taste.

To serve, halve the ox cheeks and reheat in the reduced sauce. Pan-fry the ox tongue with the butter and some seasoning until lightly browned. Divide the ox tongue between warm plates and top with the braised ox cheeks. Serve with horseradish pommes purée, ginger carrots and caper raisin purée.

# ginger carrots {6-8 servings}

1kg baby carrots, trimmed
1 tsp ground ginger
1 tsp fine sea salt
100g butter

Blanch the carrots in a pan of boiling salted water for 2–3 minutes until just tender. Meanwhile, mix the ginger and salt together in a small bowl. Drain the carrots and refresh under cold running water.

Just before serving, melt the butter in a pan. When it is foaming, add the carrots and sauté for 1–2 minutes until golden and heated through. Drain off the excess butter, sprinkle with the ginger salt and serve.

# caper raisin purée {Makes about 180ml}

50g capers, rinsed and drained
50g raisins

Put the capers and raisins in a small saucepan and pour on just enough water to cover. Bring to a simmer and cook gently for 5–10 minutes until the raisins are soft and plump. Drain the capers and raisins, reserving the liquid. Whiz them in a food processor with half the liquid to a fine purée, stopping the machine to scrape down the sides of the processor once or twice. Add a little more water if the purée is too thick.

Warm through slightly before serving.

# salad of ox tongue
## with gremolata and pecorino {Serves 4 as a starter}

½ poached ox tongue (page 144)
1 banana shallot, peeled and sliced into rings
sea salt and black pepper

**GREMOLATA:**
2 garlic cloves, peeled and chopped
finely grated zest of 1 lemon
squeeze of lemon juice
handful of flat-leaf parsley, leaves only, chopped
4–6 tbsp olive oil

**TO SERVE:**
pecorino shavings  |  handful of cress or young rocket leaves

Wrap the ox tongue in cling film and put into the freezer for 1–2 hours until firm.
Unwrap and slice as thinly as possible, using a strong, sharp knife. Overlap the slices on
individual serving plates and scatter over the shallot rings and some salt. Set aside.

To make the gremolata, crush the garlic with a pinch of salt, using a pestle and
mortar. Mix in the lemon zest, lemon juice and parsley, then stir in the olive oil, adding
less if you prefer the gremolata as a paste, or more if you like it as a dressing. Adjust the
seasoning, adding pepper to taste.

Spoon the gremolata over the tongue slices and scatter over the pecorino shavings and
cress to serve.

THIS ITALIAN SALAD *makes
a great starter. Gremolata is a
brilliant zesty dressing that works
well here, but is equally good
scattered over grilled fish, lamb
or vegetables.*

# braised ox cheeks in red wine
## with mash and bacon {Serves 4 as a main course}

4 braised ox cheeks (page 144)

2 tbsp olive oil

20g butter

200g pancetta lardons

200g baby button mushrooms or girolles

small handful of flat-leaf parsley, chopped

**BRAISED BABY ONIONS:**

1 tbsp olive oil

30g butter

20 baby pearl onions, peeled

1 tsp caster sugar

100–200ml chicken stock (page 243)

**TO SERVE:**

silky mash (page 97)

**DEEP-FRIED ONION RINGS:**

1 onion, peeled and sliced into rings

200ml whole milk

3–4 tbsp plain flour

sea salt and black pepper

groundnut or vegetable oil, for deep-frying

For the braised baby onions, heat a small pan, then add the olive oil and butter. Tip in the onions and fry for 4–5 minutes until golden brown all over. Add the sugar, toss well and cook for a couple more minutes until the sugar has caramelised. Carefully strain off the excess butter from the pan and add the chicken stock. Increase the heat and boil until the stock has reduced to a syrupy glaze. Pierce the onions with a metal skewer to check that they are tender. If not, add more stock to the pan and boil again until reduced to a glaze.

For the deep-fried onion rings, soak the onion in the milk for 30 seconds; drain well. Mix the flour with a little salt and pepper on a shallow plate. Heat the groundnut oil in deep-fat fryer or other deep, heavy pan to 170°C. Toss the onion rings in the flour to coat and shake off the excess. Add to the oil and deep-fry until golden and crisp. Drain on a tray lined with kitchen paper and sprinkle lightly with salt. Keep warm in a low oven.

Reheat the braised ox cheeks and silky mash. Heat the olive oil and butter in a pan and sauté the pancetta and mushrooms over a medium heat for 3–4 minutes until the pancetta is golden brown. Add the braised onions and toss for another minute or two until warmed through. Finally, toss in the chopped parsley and take off the heat.

Divide the ox cheeks, braised onions, mushrooms and pancetta between warm plates. Spoon the mash alongside and garnish with the deep-fried onion rings to serve.

venison with
pickled red cabbage
and butternut squash
purée

honey-roasted ham
hock with red
cabbage and piccalilli

butternut squash
risotto with toasted
walnuts

# venison with pickled red cabbage and butternut squash purée {Serves 6 as a main course}

6 portions of boned loin of venison, about
   100g each, trimmed, trimmings reserved
25g butter
sea salt and black pepper

**RED WINE SAUCE:**
1 tbsp olive oil
venison trimmings (optional)
1 shallot, peeled and sliced
½ garlic clove, peeled and chopped
1 thyme sprig
2 white peppercorns
1 bay leaf, split
1 tbsp sherry vinegar
375ml red wine
400ml chicken stock (page 243)

**TO SERVE:**
pickled red cabbage (opposite)   |   butternut squash purée (opposite)
toasted walnuts (opposite)

For the red wine sauce, heat the oil in a pan and caramelise the venison trimmings (if you have them). Add the shallot and garlic and colour lightly, then add the thyme, peppercorns and bay leaf. Continue to cook until everything is nicely golden brown. Deglaze with the sherry vinegar, then add the wine and reduce until syrupy. Add the chicken stock, bring to the boil and simmer for 20 minutes. Pass the sauce through a very fine sieve (or one lined with muslin) into a clean pan and boil to reduce to the required consistency. Season with salt and pepper to taste. Keep hot.

To cook the venison, heat the butter in a heavy-based pan. Add the venison portions, season and sear on all sides to colour beautifully all round, keeping them nice and pink in the centre. The meat should feel slightly springy when pressed. Depending on size, this should take 5–10 minutes.

Let the meat rest for a few minutes, then cut into thick slices. Put a generous spoonful of hot pickled cabbage on each warm serving plate and arrange the venison on top. Drizzle over some of the red wine sauce. Spoon some butternut squash purée alongside and add a few toasted walnuts. Serve immediately, with the remaining sauce.

# pickled red cabbage {8-10 servings}

1 medium red cabbage
150g butter
15 juniper berries
1 bay leaf, split
75g demerara sugar
250ml Cabernet Sauvignon vinegar,
  or other red wine vinegar
300ml port
300ml red wine
sea salt

VENISON *is a true winter beast. Mine comes from the Finnabrogue estate in Ireland – the animals are magnificent and their flavour is second to none. Butternut squash and vanilla have a natural sweet synergy, which works brilliantly with this dish. And pickled red cabbage – a staple in my winter kitchen – is another ideal partner.*

Core and finely shred the cabbage. Melt the butter in a large saucepan, add the cabbage and sweat gently for 2–3 minutes. Tie 10 juniper berries and the bay leaf in muslin and add to the pan with the sugar, wine vinegar, port and red wine. Cook slowly for 2–3 hours until all the liquid has evaporated. Season with a little sea salt and spoon into sterilised kilner jars. Seal and keep in a cool place for 3–4 days.

Before serving, remove the bouquet garni. Warm the cabbage over a low heat until hot (or just warm). Crush the remaining 5 juniper berries and stir them through.

# butternut squash purée {6-8 servings}

1 large butternut squash, about 1kg
150g butter
1 vanilla pod, split
sea salt

Peel, deseed and dice the butternut squash. Melt the butter in a pan. Add the squash and cook without colouring for about 15 minutes over a medium heat until very soft. Whiz in a blender until smooth. Scrape the seeds from the vanilla pod and stir them into the purée. Season with salt to taste. The purée needs to be quite dry; if necessary reheat in a clean pan to reduce slightly until you have the required consistency.

# toasted walnuts {8 servings}

Melt 25g butter in a frying pan, add 100g shelled walnuts and sauté for a minute or two until lightly browned. Drain on kitchen paper and sprinkle with salt and sugar to taste.

# honey-roasted ham hock
## with red cabbage and piccalilli

2 small ham hocks
1 large onion, peeled
1 large carrot, peeled
1 leek, trimmed
1 celery stick, trimmed
4 garlic cloves, peeled
1 thyme sprig
6 white peppercorns

**GLAZE:**
40g English mustard
40g French mustard
1 tbsp honey
100g demerara sugar
handful of cloves
handful of rosemary needles

**TO SERVE:**
pickled red cabbage (page 153)  |  piccalilli (page 250)

Rinse the ham hocks well under cold running water. Chop the vegetables roughly and put them into a large saucepan with the ham hocks. Add the garlic, thyme and peppercorns and pour in enough cold water to cover the meat. Bring to the boil, then skim off any scum from the surface. Simmer, covered, for 3–5 hours until the hocks are very tender – the bone should slide easily out of the meat.

Preheat the oven to 190°C/Gas 5. Leave the hocks to cool slightly in the liquid until you can handle them, then remove and peel off the skin, leaving the fat on. Score the fat in a criss-cross pattern. (Save the stock as this makes a great base for pea and ham soup.)

For the glaze, mix together the mustards, honey and demerara sugar. Spread the mixture over the ham hocks and stud with the cloves and rosemary needles. Place in a large roasting pan and roast in the hot oven for 15–20 minutes until the glaze caramelises. Leave to rest for 5 minutes or so after roasting.

Carve the ham hocks and serve with warm pickled red cabbage and piccalilli.

# butternut squash risotto with toasted walnuts {Serves 4–6 as a starter}

100ml olive oil
2 shallots, peeled and finely chopped
300g risotto rice (carnaroli or arborio)
1 litre chicken stock (page 243) or vegetable
  stock (page 244)
6 tbsp freshly grated Parmesan
3 tbsp mascarpone
8 tbsp butternut squash purée {page 153}
100g butter, diced
sea salt and black pepper

**TO SERVE:**
Parmesan shavings | toasted walnuts (page 153) | wood sorrel or sage leaves

To make the risotto base, heat the olive oil in a saucepan and sweat the shallots for 5 minutes to soften, without colouring. Add the rice and cook, stirring, for a minute. Pour in 700ml of the stock and bring to a simmer. Cook for about 8 minutes, then drain the rice and spread out on a plate to cool. Set aside until almost ready to serve.

Finish the risotto shortly before serving. Put the par-cooked rice in a saucepan with the remaining stock. Bring to the boil and simmer until the stock is almost all absorbed and the rice grains are al dente.

Stir in the Parmesan, mascarpone and squash purée until evenly combined. Finally, add the butter cubes, stir and season with salt and pepper to taste. The consistency should be deliciously creamy.

Divide the risotto among warm plates and scatter with Parmesan shavings, toasted walnuts and wood sorrel. Serve immediately.

MAKE THIS VIBRANT, *creamy risotto when pumpkins are in the shops — from autumn through winter. Or at other times, flavour it with a spring or summer vegetable purée. It makes a great starter and you can par-cook the rice ahead, as I have here, then finish the risotto off quickly at the last minute.*

wagyu beef with
smoked pommes
purée and roasted
artichokes

beef satay with
peanut sauce
and herb salad

carpaccio of beef
with wasabi
rémoulade

# wagyu beef with smoked pommes purée and roasted artichokes {Serves 4 as a main course}

1.5kg rib of beef, preferably Wagyu
sea salt and black pepper
2 tbsp olive oil
25g butter

**ROASTED ARTICHOKES:**
8 baby artichokes
1 lemon, halved
1 garlic clove, peeled
1 thyme sprig, plus extra to garnish
25g butter

**TO SERVE:**
smoked pommes purée (opposite)

**MISO-GLAZED FOIE GRAS:**
360g foie gras
25ml sake
25ml mirin (Japanese rice wine)
20g sugar
75g miso paste

Trim the beef and cut off the flank (use for satay, page 163). Cut the rib-eye in two (save one half for carpaccio, page 164). Wrap the other half in cling film and chill.

Prepare the artichokes one at a time. First, squeeze the juice from one lemon half into a bowl of cold water. Peel off the coarse outer layer of leaves to reveal the soft inner leaves. Trim off the tops, then peel off the tough skin covering the base. Immediately immerse in the lemon water to prevent it from discolouring. Repeat with the other artichokes.

Bring a pan of salted water to the boil with the garlic, thyme and the juice from the other lemon half. Blanch the artichokes for 4–6 minutes until tender when pierced with a skewer. Drain and refresh in a bowl of iced water, then drain again. Halve the artichokes and scoop out the furry core with a small spoon. Set aside until ready to serve.

Cut the foie gras into portions, each slice about 1cm thick; chill until ready to cook. Put the sake and mirin into a pan and boil for a few minutes to burn off the alcohol, then add the sugar and stir to dissolve. Stir in the miso paste and cook over a medium heat for a minute or two until the mixture has thickened slightly. Allow to cool completely.

When ready to serve, heat the olive oil and butter in a frying pan. Season the beef and fry for 3–4 minutes on each side until browned and medium rare, basting with the butter. Remove to a warm plate to rest while you cook the artichokes and foie gras.

Season the artichokes with salt and pepper. Heat the butter in a frying pan and fry the artichokes for 2–3 minutes until golden brown at the edges. Transfer to a plate. Wipe out the pan; return to the heat. Season the foie gras slices and fry over a high heat for 30 seconds on each side. Remove and brush with the miso glaze.

To serve, cut the beef into portions and brush with the miso glaze. Place on warm serving plates and top with a slice of foie gras. Add the roasted artichokes and a spoonful of smoked pommes purée. Garnish the artichokes with thyme and spoon over the red wine sauce to serve.

## smoked pommes purée  {4-6 servings}

500g La Ratte potatoes, washed
sea salt and black pepper
200g butter
100ml double cream
50ml milk
4 drops of smoked hickory essence

Add the potatoes to a pan of salted water, bring to the boil and simmer for 20 minutes or until tender when pierced with a skewer. Drain well. Wearing rubber gloves to protect your hands, peel off the skins using a small knife while the potatoes are still hot. Mash the potatoes, using a potato ricer if you have one, then push them through a fine sieve.

Heat the butter, cream and milk in a pan until the butter has melted. Add the potatoes and stir well to mix. To get a silky smooth result, push the purée through a fine sieve once again. Stir in the smoked hickory essence and season to taste with salt and pepper.

NOTE: For horseradish pommes purée, replace the hickory essence with 1–2 tbsp horseradish sauce to taste.

JAPANESE WAGYU BEEF *is renowned for its unique marbling, succulent texture and superb, rich flavour, but it is very expensive. You can, however, use a good-quality aged beef fillet instead.*

# beef satay with peanut sauce and herb salad {Serves 4 as a starter or light lunch}

**BEEF SATAY:**
400–450g beef fillet (or reserved outer
   flank of a rib of beef (page 160)
2–3 tbsp vegetable oil
1 red chilli, deseeded and finely chopped
1 garlic clove, peeled and finely crushed
   with a pinch of sea salt
sea salt and black pepper

**PEANUT SAUCE:**
2 tbsp vegetable oil
2 large shallots, peeled and finely diced
3 garlic cloves, peeled and finely crushed
2cm piece of fresh root ginger, peeled
   and finely grated
1 red chilli, deseeded and finely chopped
1½ tbsp light soy sauce
250ml coconut milk
1 tbsp caster sugar
100g crunchy peanut butter

**TO SERVE:**
handful of mixed herbs or small salad leaves

Trim off most of the fat and the sinew from the beef. Mix the vegetable oil, chopped chilli, garlic and seasoning in a small bowl and brush this over the beef. Cover and leave to marinate in the fridge for a couple of hours or overnight.

To make the peanut sauce, heat the oil in a saucepan over a medium heat. Add the shallots and sweat for a few minutes until they begin to soften, then stir in the garlic, ginger and chilli and cook for a few more minutes. Add the soy sauce and let it bubble until almost totally reduced. Pour in the coconut milk and add the sugar, stirring to dissolve. Bring to the boil, then immediately remove from the heat and stir in the peanut butter until well blended. If you prefer the sauce thinner, stir in a little boiling water.

Take the beef out of the fridge about 15 minutes before cooking. Heat a griddle pan until it is very hot (you should be able to feel the heat rising). Griddle the beef for about 2 minutes on each side to cook it medium rare (or cook to your liking). Remove from the heat and leave to rest for 5 minutes, then cut into 2–3cm thick strips. Thread each strip onto a short wooden skewer and brush over a little of the peanut sauce.

Divide the satay between warm serving plates and top with a scattering of mixed herbs. Serve immediately, with individual bowls of peanut sauce for dipping.

# carpaccio of beef
## with wasabi rémoulade {Serves 4 as a starter}

400–500g marbled ribeye (page 160)
  or beef fillet
1½ tbsp olive oil, plus extra to drizzle
sea salt and black pepper
1–2 tsp wasabi paste
2 tbsp brown mustard seeds

**WASABI RÉMOULADE:**
1 small celeriac
1½ tsp fine sea salt
1–1½ tsp wasabi, to taste
1½ tbsp mirin (Japanese rice wine)
2 large egg yolks
1 tsp dry English mustard
1 tsp light soy sauce
250ml groundnut oil

Trim the beef to a neat log of even thickness throughout. Heat a frying pan until hot and add the olive oil. Season the beef all over with salt and pepper, then sear it in the hot pan for a minute on each side until evenly browned.

Remove the beef from the pan and leave to cool slightly, then brush all over with the wasabi paste. Tip the mustard seeds onto a tray and shake it gently to spread out the seeds. Roll the beef in the mustard seeds to coat, then wrap tightly in a double layer of cling film. Freeze for 1–2 hours until the beef is firm. (This will make it easier to slice.)

For the rémoulade, peel the celeriac and cut into thin matchsticks. Toss it with the salt, place in a colander set over a large bowl and leave to degorge for an hour. Rinse under cold running water, squeeze out the excess liquid and pat dry with kitchen paper.

For the wasabi mayonnaise, put the wasabi, mirin, egg yolks, mustard and soy sauce into a food processor and whiz to a smooth paste. With the motor running, slowly trickle in the groundnut oil; the mixture will emulsify. Season to taste with salt and pepper.

Add 3–4 tbsp of the wasabi mayonnaise to the celeriac (just enough to bind) and toss well. Use the remainder for another dish or as a dressing for seared steak.

Remove the beef from the freezer, unwrap and cut into wafer-thin slices, using a sharp knife. Overlap the slices on one large platter or individual serving plates and rub a little olive oil over the surface to give a shiny appearance. Sprinkle with a little salt and grind over some pepper, then serve with the wasabi rémoulade and grilled focaccia.

sweet

infusion of
summer berries
with fromage frais
and lime sorbet

cranachan with
raspberries

pineapple
carpaccio
with fromage frais
and lime sorbet

# infusion of summer berries
## with fromage frais and lime sorbet {Serves 4–6}

400g mixed strawberries (including
   some fraises des bois if available)
150g blueberries
150g raspberries
10 large mint leaves, finely shredded

**INFUSION:**
200ml red wine
100ml good quality red wine vinegar (we
   use Banyuls Cabernet Sauvignon)
50ml Armagnac
50g caster sugar
1 star anise
pinch of ground cumin
1 clove
150g mixed berries (e.g. blueberries,
   blackberries, raspberries)
1–2 tsp icing sugar, to taste

**TO SERVE:**
fromage frais and lime sorbet (opposite)  |  pinch of vanilla salt (opposite)

First, prepare the infusion. Pour the red wine and wine vinegar into a pan, add the Armagnac, sugar and spices, and bring to a simmer. Meanwhile, whiz the berries in a food processor to a fine purée, then push through a fine sieve to remove the seeds. As the infusion liquor begins to boil, remove the pan from the heat and leave to cool completely. Strain the cooled liquor through a sieve, then mix with the berry purée. Taste and adjust the sweetness, adding a little icing sugar to balance the acidity as necessary.

Hull the strawberries and quarter or halve large ones. Place in a bowl with the blueberries and raspberries. Add the shredded mint and toss gently to mix. Divide the berries among glass serving bowls and pour the berry infusion into a serving jug.

To serve, top each serving with a scoop of fromage frais and lime sorbet and sprinkle with a little vanilla salt. Pour the berry infusion over the fruit.

# fromage frais and lime sorbet

{Makes about 1.5 litres}

500ml water
225g liquid glucose
250g caster sugar
285g fromage frais
finely pared zest and juice of 5 limes

Put the water, liquid glucose and sugar into a pan and stir over a low heat until the sugar has dissolved. Increase the heat and bring the syrup to the boil. Immediately remove the pan from the heat and leave to cool completely.

Put the fromage frais into a large bowl and beat lightly to loosen it. Gradually mix in the cooled sugar syrup. Stir in the lime zest and juice, cover the bowl with cling film and chill for a few hours or overnight.

Pass the mixture through a fine sieve and discard the lime zest. Transfer it to an ice-cream machine and churn until almost firm. Scoop the sorbet into a shallow container and freeze for 4–6 hours until firm.

# vanilla salt

Split 2 vanilla pods lengthways and scrape out the seeds with the back of a knife. Tip them into a mortar and add 1 tsp coarse sea salt. Grind together using a pestle until evenly combined.

# cranachan with raspberries

70g oatmeal
170g raspberries
1–2 tbsp icing sugar, to taste
700ml double cream
4 tbsp runny honey
2–3 tbsp malt whisky, to taste

Lightly toast the oatmeal in a dry frying pan over a medium heat until lightly golden, tossing frequently. (Do not leave the pan unattended as the oatmeal is liable to burn easily.) Tip onto a flat plate and leave to cool completely.

Put 100g of the raspberries and the icing sugar into a blender or food processor and whiz to a smooth purée. In a large bowl, whip the cream to soft peaks, then fold in the honey and whisky. Set aside 1–2 tbsp of the oatmeal for serving and fold the rest into the cream mixture. Spoon 1 tbsp of the raspberry purée into the base of each serving glass. Add the rest to the cream mixture and give it two or three folds to create a rippled effect.

Fill the serving glasses with the oatmeal and cream mixture. Top with the remaining raspberries and sprinkle over the reserved oatmeal. Serve at once.

THIS SCOTTISH DESSERT *is incredibly easy to put together – perfect when you're entertaining and prefer to concentrate on having a good time with your guests. You can also make it with blackberries when they are in season – just add a little extra honey, as they tend to be a bit tart – and sieve out the seeds for a smooth purée.*

# pineapple carpaccio
## with fromage frais and lime sorbet {Serves 4-6}

1 ripe medium pineapple
250ml vanilla sugar syrup (page 240), cooled

**TO SERVE:**

fromage frais and lime sorbet (page 171) | finely grated zest of 1 lime
pinch of finely crushed mixed peppercorns

Peel the pineapple by slicing off the top and bottom, then cutting away the peel along the length of the fruit. Prise out the 'eyes' with the tip of the knife. Turn the pineapple on its side and cut into wafer-thin slices, preferably using a sharp fruit knife. Add the slices to the cooled vanilla syrup and chill for at least an hour or overnight.

Heat the oven to its lowest setting. Line a baking tray with a silicone liner. Pick out 4–6 neat pineapple slices and use a small pastry cutter to stamp out the core. Place the pineapple rings on the lined baking tray in a single layer. Let them dry out in the low oven for up to 2–2½ hours until they are firm and can be lifted off the silicone easily. If not using immediately, store the cooled pineapple rings in a small airtight container, interleaved with discs of baking parchment.

When ready to serve, remove the macerated pineapple slices from the fridge and drain, reserving the vanilla syrup.

For a smart assembly, press 4 or 5 macerated pineapple slices into a slim rectangular mould so that they form a row of tiny cups along the length of the mould. Invert onto a serving plate, remove the mould and sprinkle with the lime zest and crushed peppercorns. Place a scoop of fromage frais and lime sorbet on a marinated pineapple disc alongside and carefully position a dried pineapple ring on top. Drizzle with the reserved vanilla syrup and serve immediately.

**NOTE:** For a simple presentation, omit the dried pineapple slices. Arrange the fresh pineapple slices on individual serving plates, add a scoop of sorbet and drizzle with the vanilla syrup to serve.

mango parfait with
orange anise jelly

candied oranges
with orange jelly and
chantilly cream

mango soup with
lychee granita

# mango parfait
## with orange anise jelly {Serves 6}

**MANGO PARFAIT:**

3 large, ripe, but firm mangoes

3 large egg yolks

75g caster sugar

180g double cream

**TO SERVE:**

mango sorbet (opposite) | orange and star anise jelly (opposite) | orange powder (opposite)

finely ground star anise | coriander shoots or sprigs (optional)

First, prepare the moulds. Place six 7–8cm round metal cutters on a flat tray and line with cling film. (If you don't have enough metal cutters, line a small cake tin instead.)

Peel the mangoes and cut the flesh away from the stone in thin, wide slices. From the larger slices, stamp out 6 neat discs using an 8–9cm cutter, then cut out another 6 discs, using a 7–8cm cutter. Lay on a plate, wrap with cling film and chill until ready to serve.

Roughly chop the rest of the mango and trimmings. Whiz to a purée in a blender or food processor. Push the purée through a fine sieve and discard the fibrous pulp. Measure out 250g of the purée and set aside. (Use the rest for another dish or to make a smoothie.)

Put the egg yolks and sugar in a large heatproof bowl and beat lightly to mix. Set the bowl over a pan of barely simmering water (making sure the base of the bowl isn't in contact with the water). Whisk the mixture using a hand-held electric whisk until it triples in volume and becomes thick and pale. When you lift the beaters, the mixture should be thick enough to leave a ribbon trail across the surface.

Lightly whip the cream in another bowl to soft peaks. Carefully fold the mango purée into the whisked egg mixture, then fold in the whipped cream. Divide between the prepared moulds (or spoon into the lined cake tin). Cover them with a large sheet of cling film and freeze until firm.

To serve, unmould the individual mango parfaits (or use a 7–8cm metal cutter to cut out neat portions if you've frozen the parfait in one large mould). Place a larger mango disc on each serving plate and top with a parfait. Lay a smaller mango disc on the parfait. Rest a quenelle of mango sorbet and a spoonful of orange jelly on top. Sprinkle a little orange powder and ground star anise onto the jellies, and finish with coriander if you like. Serve at once.

# orange and star anise jelly {6 servings}

250ml fresh orange juice, strained
2 star anise
2 sheets of leaf gelatine

Gently heat the orange juice with the star anise in a pan to a bare simmer. Meanwhile, soak the gelatine in cold water to cover for a few minutes to soften. Drain the gelatine, squeeze out excess water, then add to the orange juice, off the heat, and stir to dissolve. Strain through a fine sieve into a rigid plastic container. Let cool, then chill until set.

# mango sorbet {6 servings}

2 large or 3 medium mangoes
75ml light sugar syrup (page 240)
25g liquid glucose
juice of 1 lime

Peel the mangoes and cut the flesh from the stone, then chop roughly. Whiz in a blender or food processor to a smooth purée, then pass through a fine sieve into a large bowl and discard the fibrous pulp. Measure 500g of the mango purée (use the rest for a smoothie).

Bring the sugar syrup and glucose to a simmer in a pan, stirring until evenly combined. Let cool, then mix with the lime juice and mango purée. Pour into an ice-cream machine and churn until almost firm. Transfer to a shallow container and freeze until solid.

# orange powder {Makes 2–3 tbsp}

2 large oranges

Thinly pare the zest from the oranges, using a swivel vegetable peeler and cut away any white pith from it with a small sharp knife. Blanch the zest in a pan of boiling water for a few seconds, then immediately refresh in iced water. Repeat this two or three times as it will help to remove the bitterness from the zest. Drain and pat dry with kitchen paper.

Heat the oven to its lowest setting, about 100°C/Gas ¼. Spread the zest out on a baking sheet and dry out in the oven for about 30–40 minutes until crisp and brittle. You should be able to scrunch the zest into small pieces. Whiz in a food processor or spice grinder to a fine powder. Sift to remove any large bits and store in an airtight container.

FOR THIS *elegant, simple dessert, you can prepare the oranges well in advance and keep them immersed in the syrup. Use vanilla pods from Madagascar if you can find them — they are the plumpest of all the vanilla pods and the most potent.*

# candied oranges with orange jelly and chantilly cream {Serves 6-8}

**CANDIED ORANGES:**

2 medium oranges, washed

500g caster sugar

600ml water

**CHANTILLY CREAM:**

300ml double cream

1 vanilla pod, split and seeds scraped

1–2 tbsp icing sugar, to taste

**TO SERVE:**

1–2 empty vanilla pods, sliced (optional)

orange and star anise jelly (page 179)

orange powder, to sprinkle (optional)

few star anise

Put the oranges into the freezer for 20 minutes to firm them up slightly. Cut off the top and bottom of each one and slice the oranges as thinly as possible – the slices should be about 2mm thick.

Bring the kettle to the boil and have a bowl of iced water ready on the side. Put the orange slices into a large heatproof bowl, pour over enough boiling water to cover and leave for a minute. Carefully pour off the hot water, then briefly refresh the orange slices in the iced water and remove. Repeat blanching and refreshing the orange slices twice. This will draw out the bitter edge from the orange skins. Drain well.

Put the sugar and water into a heavy-based pan and stir over a low heat to dissolve the sugar. Increase the heat, bring to the boil and let bubble for a few minutes. Reduce the heat to low and add the blanched orange slices. Lay a crumpled piece of greaseproof paper on top and cook gently for 1–1¼ hours until the orange slices are translucent and tender. You may need to add a little water to the pan halfway through cooking if the syrup becomes too thick.

Transfer to a bowl and allow to cool completely, then chill for about 10 minutes. (The candied orange slices keep well covered with the syrup in a sealed container in the fridge for a month or longer.)

When ready to serve, for the Chantilly cream, lightly whip the cream with the vanilla seeds and icing sugar to taste. Slice the vanilla pods if using as a decoration. Place 2 orange slices on each serving plate, and sprinkle with a little orange powder if you like. Place a spoonful of orange and star anise jelly on one orange slice and a spoonful of Chantilly cream on the other. Top with the star anise and sliced vanilla pods, if using. Serve at once.

# mango soup with lychee granita {Serves 4}

**MANGO SOUP:**
2–3 large overripe mangoes
200–250ml lychee juice
200ml light sugar syrup (page 240)

**LYCHEE ICE CUBES:**
400g can lychees in syrup
few mint leaves, shredded

**LYCHEE GRANITA:**
500ml lychee juice

**TO SERVE:**
drizzle of sugar syrup (optional)   |   handful of baby mint leaves

First, make the lychee ice cubes. Drain the lychees and reserve the syrup. Put one lychee and a little shredded mint into each compartment of an ice-cube tray. Fill the tray with the reserved syrup and freeze until solid.

For the lychee granita, pour the lychee juice into a wide shallow container and freeze for 2–3 hours until semi-frozen. Scrape the granita with a metal spoon to loosen the ice crystals around the edges and mix them into the still-liquid centre (but don't beat, as you want to achieve a granular texture). Return to the freezer for a few more hours.

For the mango soup, peel the mangoes and cut the flesh away from the stone. Chop roughly and whiz to a smooth purée in a blender or food processor. Mix in 200ml lychee juice and the sugar syrup, adding a little more lychee juice as necessary to get the desired consistency. Pass the purée through a fine sieve and discard the fibrous pulp.

To serve, pour the mango soup into chilled bowls and drizzle with a little sugar syrup if you like. Scrape the lychee granita with a strong metal spoon and place on one side of each bowl. Scatter the baby mint leaves over the granita and serve immediately, with a few lychee ice cubes on the side.

ALFONSO MANGOES *are particularly flavourful – ideal for this easy dessert, though any very ripe mango will do. The lychee ice cubes are a bit of extra fun and a talking point at the table, but of course they are optional.*

coconut pannacotta
with white chocolate
granita and black
olive caramel

pannacotta with
poached fruits in
champagne syrup

macerated
strawberries with
clotted cream and
black olive caramel

# coconut pannacotta with white chocolate granita and black olive caramel {Serves 6}

**COCONUT PANNACOTTA:**

2 sheets of leaf gelatine
100g white chocolate, chopped
600g coconut purée or coconut cream

**MANGO PURÉE:**

1 medium ripe mango
icing sugar, to taste (optional)

**TO SERVE:**

white chocolate granita (opposite) | pinch of vanilla salt (page 171)
black olive caramel (opposite) | sablé biscuits (page 212), optional

To make the pannacottas, soak the gelatine in cold water to cover for about 5 minutes to soften. Meanwhile, gently melt the white chocolate in a heatproof bowl set over a pan of hot water. Warm the coconut purée in a pan until almost simmering, then remove from the heat. When the chocolate has melted, take off the heat and stir until smooth.

Squeeze the gelatine to remove excess water, then add to the hot coconut purée, stirring until melted. Pour on to the chocolate, whisking until smooth. Pass through a fine sieve into a jug and leave to cool slightly. Pour the pannacotta mixture into small serving glasses. Allow to cool, then chill in the fridge for 8 hours or overnight until set.

For the mango purée, peel the mango and cut the flesh away from the stone, then whiz in a blender until smooth. Sweeten with a little icing sugar, if required. Pass through a fine sieve into a bowl and chill.

To serve, spoon a little mango purée on top of each pannacotta. Scrape shavings from the white chocolate granita block using a strong spoon and place on top of the mango purée. Sprinkle with a little vanilla salt. Drizzle a teaspoonful of black olive caramel over each portion and serve immediately, with sablé biscuits if you like.

THIS UNUSUAL DESSERT *was
again inspired by my time at
El Bulli. Coconut and mango give
classic Italian pannacotta an Asian
slant and the caramel brings the
flavours together brilliantly. Black
olive caramel may sound wild, but
it is truly amazing, so do give it a
try! Sprinkling a little vanilla salt
on top, as you serve the dish, sets
the tastebuds tingling.*

# white chocolate granita
{Makes 375g, about 6 servings}

100g white chocolate
75ml whipping cream
200ml water

Melt the white chocolate gently in a heatproof bowl set over a pan of hot water. Stir until smooth and remove from the heat. Mix in the cream and water. Pass through a fine sieve into a deep metal tray and freeze for 2–3 hours until semi-frozen.

Scrape the granita with a metal spoon to loosen the texture, then return to the freezer until ready to serve.

# black olive caramel
{Makes about 350g, up to 24 servings}

200g caster sugar
50g liquid glucose
100g black olive paste (finely blended pitted olives)

Melt the sugar with the glucose in a heavy-based pan over a low heat, then increase the heat and boil to a light golden caramel. Take off the heat and let cool slightly, then whisk in the olive paste. Leave to cool completely.

Store the caramel in a corked bottle or screw-topped jar in the fridge. It will keep for a month or longer.

# pannacotta with poached fruits in champagne syrup {Serves 6}

6 coconut pannacottas (page 186)

**CHAMPAGNE SYRUP:**

600ml Champagne

400g sugar

16g fresh root ginger, peeled and sliced

2 pinches of ground cinnamon

1 vanilla pod, split and seeds scraped

**FRUITS:**

12 strawberries, halved or quartered depending on size

2 kiwi fruits, peeled and sliced

1 mango, peeled, stoned and sliced

8 lychees, peeled

4 very thin slices of pineapple, peeled and cored

**TO SERVE:**

pinch of vanilla salt (page 171) | 1 vanilla pod, finely sliced lengthways

To prepare the syrup, put the Champagne, sugar, ginger, cinnamon and vanilla pod in a pan and bring to the boil. Reduce the heat and simmer for 5 minutes to allow the flavours to infuse. Strain the syrup through a fine sieve.

Return a quarter of the syrup to the pan, add the strawberries and bring to the boil. Immediately remove from the heat, tip into a bowl and set aside to cool. Repeat with the kiwi and mango in turn. Add the lychees and pineapple to the remaining quarter of syrup, bring to the boil and simmer for 2 minutes, then remove from the heat and cool.

To serve, drain the fruit; strain and reserve the liquor. Turn out the pannacottas into shallow serving bowls and arrange the fruit around them. Drizzle the Champagne syrup over the fruit to glaze and finish with a sprinkling of vanilla salt and a sliver of vanilla pod. Serve immediately.

VARY THE FRUITS *for this simple dessert according to the season. Make the pannacottas in little individual moulds (so you can turn them out) and macerate the fruits in the syrup well in advance.*

*The poached fruits are delicious enough to serve on their own with crème fraîche. Alternatively, save any that are leftover for breakfast the next morning – pile on to slices of hot brioche and top with a dollop of mascarpone.*

# macerated strawberries with clotted cream and black olive caramel {Serves 4}

500g strawberries, hulled
100g caster sugar
100ml water
1 vanilla pod, split and seeds scraped
4 black peppercorns, crushed

**TO SERVE:**
clotted cream | pinch of vanilla salt (page 171) | black olive caramel (page 187)

Halve or quarter the strawberries depending on size and place in a large bowl. Put the sugar and water in a large pan and slowly bring to the boil to dissolve the sugar, then add the vanilla pod and seeds, and crushed peppercorns. Remove from the heat and pour the syrup over the strawberries. Leave to macerate in a warm place for 15 minutes.

To serve, drain the strawberries, removing the vanilla pod and peppercorns. Cut 4 wafer-thin strips from the vanilla pod. Arrange the strawberries on large plates, add a generous scoop of clotted cream and sprinkle with a little vanilla salt. Drizzle the berries and cream with black olive caramel and lay a vanilla pod sliver on the cream to finish.

WHEN I WAS A SMALL BOY, *I used to pick strawberries in Lincolnshire to earn pocket money. I'd take them home and mum would make wonderful crumbles to eat with clotted cream. The start of the English strawberry season is still special for me ... and I've discovered that black olive caramel works brilliantly with my favourite strawberries and clotted cream.*

apple trifle with cider granita and doughnuts

apple crumble with hazelnuts and caramel custard

doughnuts with apple filling and chocolate sauce

# apple trifle with cider granita
## and doughnuts {Serves 10-12}

**APPLE JELLY:**
5 Granny Smith apples
pinch of vitamin C powder (or 1 tsp lemon juice)
150ml water
250ml sugar syrup (page 240)
5 gelatine leaves

**CUSTARD LAYER:**
600ml caramel custard

**CALVADOS CREAM:**
250ml whipping cream
1–2 tbsp icing sugar, to taste
1–2 tbsp Calvados, to taste

**TO SERVE:**
cider granita (opposite)　|　apple doughnuts (page 198)

For the jelly, quarter and core the apples, then juice them using a juice extractor. You should have about 500ml of juice. Mix with the vitamin C powder or lemon juice, water and half the sugar syrup.

Soak the gelatine leaves in cold water to cover for 5 minutes to soften. Meanwhile, heat the remaining sugar syrup in a small pan until it just begins to simmer. Remove the pan from the heat. Drain the gelatine and squeeze out the excess water, then add to the pan and stir to dissolve. Pass through a sieve into a large bowl.

Stir in the apple juice mixture until the combined liquid is well mixed. Strain it through a fine sieve into a large jug. Pour into individual small serving glasses to one-third fill them and chill for 6 hours or overnight until set. Spoon a generous layer of cold caramel custard over the set apple jellies and chill.

To make the Calvados cream, whip the cream and icing sugar in a bowl to soft peaks, then fold in the Calvados to taste. Spoon a thin layer over the caramel custards and chill.

When ready to serve, scrape the cider granita with a strong spoon and place heaped spoonfuls on top of the apple trifles. Serve with a few apple doughnuts on the side.

# cider granita {10-12 servings, or 6-8 as a stand-alone dessert}

500ml cider (preferably Magners)
210ml sugar syrup (page 240)
210ml apple juice (juiced from 2–3 apples)

Combine all the ingredients in a large bowl. Strain the mixture through a fine sieve into a shallow freezerproof container and freeze for 1–2 hours until partially frozen. Stir the ice crystals around the sides of the container into the still-liquid centre (but do not beat). Return to the freezer for 4–6 hours. Scrape the granita with a strong spoon to serve.

# caramel custard {Makes 600ml}

165g caster sugar
150ml double cream
375ml whole milk
1 vanilla pod, split and seeds scraped (optional)
25g cornflour
4 large egg yolks

First, make the caramel. Heat a heavy-based pan until it is very hot. Gradually add 100g of the sugar, a little at a time, so that it melts immediately on contact with the hot pan. As the sugar melts and caramelises, tilt the pan to swirl and mix the caramel. When the caramel turns a dark terracotta colour, pour in 100ml of the cream, protecting your hand from the steam with an oven glove. Tilt the pan again to mix the cream with the caramel. Remove from the heat and pour through a fine sieve into a wide bowl. Leave to cool completely.

Put the milk, and vanilla seeds if using, into a pan and slowly bring to a simmer. Meanwhile, mix the remaining 65g sugar and the cornflour together in a large bowl. Add the egg yolks and beat to a smooth paste, then stir in the remaining 50ml cream. Just as the milk begins to bubble up the sides of the pan, take off the heat and slowly pour it onto the egg yolk mixture, stirring continuously. Strain the mixture through a fine sieve into a clean pan and stir over a low heat until thickened. Increase the heat and bring to the boil, stirring all the while. Simmer, stirring, for 4–5 minutes to cook out the cornflour.

Pass the custard through a fine sieve into a bowl and cover the surface with cling film to prevent a skin from forming. Allow to cool completely. Once cooled, mix the caramel into the custard, using a hand-held stick blender, until smooth.

MADE WITH *Bramley* apples, this has always been a great British pudding. I like to jazz up the topping with hazelnuts to give it more texture, and serve the crumble with a luxurious custard enriched with caramel.

# apple crumble with hazelnuts
## and caramel custard {Serves 4-6}

**APPLE COMPOTE:**
juice of 1 lemon
2kg Bramley apples
300g caster sugar
50g unsalted butter
1–2 spent vanilla pods, i.e. with
    their seeds scraped out (optional)

**CRUMBLE:**
100g plain flour
50g granulated sugar
pinch of ground cinnamon
50g unsalted cold butter, diced
50g toasted hazelnuts, lightly crushed

**TO SERVE:**
caramel custard (page 195), warmed

First, prepare the apple compote. Add the lemon juice to a large bowl of cold water. Working with one at a time, peel, core and chop the apples and immediately immerse in the bowl of lemon water to prevent them from discolouring. Drain well and pat dry with kitchen paper.

Put the chopped apples in a wide pan with the sugar, butter and vanilla pod(s) if using. Cook over a medium-low heat for 15–20 minutes until the apples are just soft, but still just holding their shape. Remove the vanilla pod(s). (If making the apple doughnuts on page 198, reserve a quarter of the compote for the filling; otherwise use it all for the crumble.)

Spoon the apple compote into a shallow ovenproof dish, about 23cm in diameter, and leave to cool completely.

For the crumble, put the flour, sugar, cinnamon and butter into a food processor and pulse for a few seconds until the mixture resembles fine breadcrumbs. Alternatively, rub the butter into the dry mixture with your fingers. Stir in the crushed hazelnuts, then spread a layer of crumble over the apple filling. Chill until ready to cook.

Preheat the oven to 200°C/Gas 6. Stand the dish on a baking sheet and bake for about 20–25 minutes until golden brown and crisp on top. Spoon into individual bowls and serve with warm caramel custard.

# doughnuts with apple filling
## and chocolate sauce {Makes about 20}

**DOUGHNUTS:**

250g plain flour, plus extra to dust

1 tsp sea salt

25g caster sugar

15g fresh yeast (or 7g sachet fast-action dried)

40ml whole milk

1 large egg, lightly beaten

½ tbsp dark rum

½ tbsp rosewater

40g butter, softened to room temperature

¼ quantity apple compote (page 197)

groundnut or sunflower oil, for deep-frying

**CINNAMON SUGAR:**

100g caster sugar

1 tsp ground cinnamon

**CHOCOLATE SAUCE:**

250g dark chocolate, in small pieces

125ml warm sugar syrup (page 240)

To make the doughnuts, put the flour, salt and sugar into a free-standing electric mixer fitted with a dough hook, stir to combine and make a well in the centre. Stir the yeast and milk together until creamy and add to the well. Add the egg, rum and rosewater. Mix on low speed to combine, then increase the speed slightly and mix until the dough comes together in a ball. Mix in the butter, a little at a time, until fully incorporated and the dough is smooth. If it seems too wet, mix in a little more flour, a spoonful at a time.

Transfer the dough to a lightly oiled bowl, cover with cling film and leave to prove slowly in the fridge overnight, by which time the dough should have doubled in size.

Purée the apple compote in a blender, pass through a sieve into a pan and stir over a high heat until thick. Cool slightly, then spoon into a piping bag fitted with a slim nozzle.

Knock back the dough and knead it lightly on a floured surface. Divide in two and roll each portion into a long log, about 3–4cm in diameter. Cut into 20–25g pieces and place, well apart, on an oiled baking sheet. Cover with lightly oiled cling film and leave to prove in a warm place for 1–2 hours until the doughnuts have almost doubled in size.

For the cinnamon sugar, mix the sugar and spice together and scatter on a deep plate. For the chocolate sauce, melt the chocolate in a heatproof bowl set over a pan of barely simmering water. Stir until smooth, then remove from the heat and stir in the sugar syrup; keep warm.

Heat the oil in a deep-fat fryer or deep, heavy pan to 190°C. In small batches, deep-fry the doughnuts until golden brown all over. Remove with a slotted spoon to a tray lined with kitchen paper. While still warm, pipe the apple purée into their centres and toss the doughnuts in cinnamon sugar to coat. Keep warm in a low oven while you finish the rest. Serve the warm doughnuts immediately, with the chocolate sauce for dipping.

marinated peaches
with basil sorbet and
strawberry jelly

peach and cherry
salad with pistachio
milk shake

strawberry jelly
with fromage frais
sorbet

# marinated peaches with
# basil sorbet and strawberry jelly {Serves 4-6}

**MARINATED PEACHES:**

2 ripe peaches

1 quantity vanilla sugar syrup (page 240)

**BASIL SORBET:**

200g liquid glucose

65g caster sugar

550ml water

juice of 1 ½ lemons

80g basil leaves

**TO SERVE:**

2 handfuls of strawberries (ideally ½ Gariguette, ½ fraises des bois (wild strawberries), hulled
strawberry jelly (opposite)　|　cracked or grated Sarawak pepper or black peppercorns
crystallised coriander or basil leaves, to finish

First, make the basil sorbet. Put the liquid glucose, sugar and water into a saucepan and stir over a low heat until the sugar has dissolved. Increase the heat and boil the syrup for a few minutes, then pour into a wide bowl and leave to cool completely.

Put the syrup, lemon juice and basil into a blender and whiz until the basil is finely ground and the syrup is bright green. Strain through a fine sieve into an ice-cream machine and churn until almost firm. Turn into a freezerproof container and freeze until firm.

To prepare the marinated peaches, halve the peaches and prise out the stones, then slice into thin rounds. Place them in a bowl and pour over the vanilla sugar syrup to coat. Wrap the bowl with cling film and chill for at least 20 minutes.

To serve, line each serving plate with a layer of marinated peach slices and spoon over a little vanilla syrup. Cut the Gariguette strawberries in half and scatter them over the peaches, cut side up. Top each strawberry half with a teaspoonful of strawberry jelly and sprinkle a little grated or crushed Sarawak pepper on top. Dot a few fraises des bois around each plate and finish with a crystallised coriander leaf. Finally, place a neat scoop of basil sorbet on each plate and serve immediately.

**NOTE:** Sarawak pepper ( shown in the previous photograph) has a sweet fragrance and a distinctive flavour. It is available from delicatessens and online.

# strawberry jelly {4-6 servings}

900g very ripe or frozen strawberries, hulled
60g caster sugar
150ml sugar syrup (page 240)
2 or 3 spent vanilla pods, i.e. with their seeds
    scraped out
2 lemon thyme sprigs
5 sheets of leaf gelatine

Roughly chop the strawberries and put them into a deep heatproof bowl with the sugar, sugar syrup, vanilla pods and thyme. Mix well, then cover the bowl with cling film and stand it over a pan of barely simmering water. Cook gently for 40–50 minutes until the strawberries are soft and have released their juices.

Just before the strawberries will be ready, soak the gelatine in cold water to cover for 5 minutes. Remove the bowl from the pan and strain the strawberries through a fine sieve into a clean bowl. Measure 500ml of juice for the jelly. (If you have more, save it to make a smoothie.)

If the juice has cooled down significantly, warm it up in a small saucepan. Drain the gelatine and squeeze out the excess water, then add to the strawberry juice and stir to dissolve. Strain through a fine sieve into a rigid plastic container. Cool completely, then chill for 8 hours or overnight until set.

# crystallised herb leaves

handful of herb leaves, such as coriander, basil,
    mint or flat-leaf parsley
1 large egg white
about 50g caster sugar

Wash the herb leaves carefully, lay them out on a piece of kitchen paper and pat dry with another piece of kitchen paper. Line a baking tray with a silicone liner or baking parchment. Lightly beat the egg white in a small bowl. Scatter the caster sugar on a plate.

Dip each leaf into the egg white, then into the caster sugar to coat. Lay on the lined tray and leave to dry out in a warm part of the kitchen or in an airing cupboard. Store in an airtight container unless using immediately.

THIS SUMMER FRUIT *and pistachio salad is easy, and the drink is optional. In the restaurant we serve the milk shake with vanilla straws, made by threading a wooden skewer through trimmed, soft, pliable vanilla pods repeatedly to widen the hollow. The straws need to be left to dry out slightly before using.*

# peach and cherry salad
## with pistachio milk shake {Serves 6}

**PEACH AND CHERRY SALAD:**

2 ripe peaches
350g ripe cherries
250ml vanilla sugar syrup (page 240)
handful of roasted and skinned pistachio nuts, roughly chopped

**PISTACHIO MILK SHAKE:**

300ml vanilla crème anglaise (page 241)
125g roasted and skinned pistachio nuts
150ml sugar syrup (page 240)
100ml water
200ml milk

Halve the peaches and prise out the stones, then cut into bite-sized pieces. Cut the cherries in half and remove the stones. Put the fruit into a bowl, add the vanilla sugar syrup and chopped pistachios, and toss to mix. Cover and leave to macerate in the fridge for at least 20 minutes.

For the milk shake, make the crème anglaise and leave to cool, stirring every once in a while to prevent a skin forming. Meanwhile, put the pistachios, sugar syrup and water into a blender and whiz for a few minutes until you have a thick, smooth mixture. Push it through a fine sieve into a large bowl. Stir in the crème anglaise and milk, adding a splash more milk if you prefer a thinner consistency. Cover with cling film and chill.

When ready to serve, divide the peaches and cherries between serving bowls. Using a hand-held stick blender, froth up the pistachio milk shake, then pour into small, individual glasses. Pop a straw (a vanilla one if you like, see opposite) into each glass and serve at once with the fruit salad.

# strawberry jelly
## with fromage frais sorbet {Serves 4}

1 quantity strawberry jelly mixture (page 203)

**FROMAGE FRAIS SORBET:**
105ml water
100g caster sugar
20g liquid glucose
400g fromage frais
juice of 1 lemon

Make up the strawberry jelly and pour into individual serving glasses. Allow to cool completely, then chill for 8 hours or overnight until firm.

To make the fromage frais sorbet, put the water, sugar and liquid glucose into a saucepan and stir over a low heat until the sugar has dissolved. Increase the heat and let the syrup boil for a couple of minutes. Now pour it into a bowl set over a larger bowl of iced water and stir every once in a while to cool it down quickly.

In another bowl, lightly beat the fromage frais with a spatula to loosen it, then stir in the lemon juice. Add the cooled sugar syrup and stir until the mixture is smooth. Pass through a fine sieve into an ice-cream machine. Churn until almost firm, then transfer to a suitable container and freeze until firm.

Transfer the sorbet to the fridge 5–10 minutes before serving to soften slightly. Top each strawberry jelly with a few small scoops of fromage frais sorbet and serve at once.

WHO SECRETLY *doesn't love jelly and ice cream? At home, we love it. This is a sophisticated version that is totally delicious. The vanilla and thyme in the jelly really lift the tart flavour of the yogurt.*

liquorice poached
pears with sorbet
tuiles

poached pears with
sablé and blackberry
sorbet

pear and star
anise bread
and butter pudding

# liquorice poached pears
## with sorbet tuiles {Serves 6}

600g caster sugar
1 litre hot water
3 liquorice sticks
3–3½ tsp liquorice essence, to taste

60g liquorice candy (e.g. Panda), finely diced
40ml crème de cassis
½ lemon
6 Williams pears

**TO SERVE:**

6 polenta tuiles (opposite)  |  pear sorbet (opposite)  |  caramel cream (page 240)
shredded basil (optional)

For the poaching syrup, put 100g of the sugar into a saucepan (large enough to take the pears). Place over a high heat to melt and caramelise the sugar. Don't move the pan until the syrup has taken on a dark caramel colour, but don't let it burn. Protecting your hand with an oven glove, take the pan off the heat and carefully pour in the hot water, standing well back as the caramel will splutter ferociously. Add the remaining sugar, liquorice sticks, 2 tsp liquorice essence, half the liquorice candy and the liqueur. Stir to dissolve the sugar and liquorice, then simmer for 5 minutes. Take off the heat and set aside to infuse.

Squeeze the lemon juice into a large bowl of cold water. One at a time, peel the pears, then immediately immerse in the bowl of lemon water. When you've finished, drain the pears and gently lower them into the liquorice syrup. Poach until tender: ripe pears only take 5–7 minutes; firmer fruit will need up to 12–15 minutes. They are ready when they begin to look translucent and can be pierced easily with a skewer. Transfer to a bowl and leave the pears to cool in the poaching syrup, then cover with cling film and chill for up to 2 days to allow the pears to take on some colour and flavour from the liquorice syrup.

For the liquorice glaze, pour 500ml of the poaching syrup into a wide pan and add the remaining 30g diced liquorice candy. Boil vigorously over a high heat until reduced to a thick syrupy consistency. Stir in ½–1 tsp liquorice essence to taste and leave to cool.

Preheat the oven to 130°C/Gas 1. Lay the polenta tuiles on a silicone-lined baking sheet and warm them in the oven for 1–2 minutes until soft and pliable. Twist around the handles of 2–3 wooden spoons to form cigar shapes. Leave to cool and firm up.

Transfer the pear sorbet to the fridge 10 minutes before serving to soften slightly, then spoon into a small disposable piping bag and place in the freezer until ready to assemble.

To serve, put a spoonful of caramel cream on each plate. Slice the pears and arrange on top. Drizzle the liquorice glaze around each plate. Pipe the sorbet into the tuile cigars and rest one on each plate. Sprinkle with a little shredded basil if you like, then serve.

# pear sorbet {Makes about 1 litre}

150g caster sugar
20g trimoline (or liquid glucose)
300ml water
juice of 1 ½ lemons
1kg ripe pears

Put the sugar, trimoline and water into a pan and stir over a low heat to dissolve the sugar. Simmer for a few minutes to thicken slightly. Cool, then add the juice of 1 lemon.

Add the remaining lemon juice to a large bowl of cold water. One at a time, peel, core and chop the pears and immerse them in the lemon water to stop them discolouring. Take out and drain half of the pears, then whiz in a blender with half of the sugar syrup to a fine purée. Push through a fine sieve into the bowl of an ice-cream machine. Repeat with the rest. Churn until almost firm, then transfer to a suitable container and freeze until firm.

# polenta tuiles {Makes about 40}

60g unsalted butter
25ml double cream
75g caster sugar
¼ tsp pectin
25g liquid glucose
70g instant polenta

Put the butter, cream, sugar, pectin and liquid glucose into a pan and stir over a low heat to dissolve the sugar and combine the glucose. Increase the heat and bring to the boil. Remove from the heat and whisk in the polenta in a slow steady stream – the mixture should be smooth and creamy. Transfer to a wide bowl and leave to cool and firm up.

Preheat the oven to 170°C/Gas 3. Roll out half of the polenta mixture between a silicone liner (beneath) and a sheet of baking parchment (on top), as thinly as possible. Peel off the paper and lift the silicone liner and tuile sheet onto a baking sheet. Bake for 12–15 minutes until golden brown. Remove from the oven and leave to cool for a minute.

Cut the tuile sheet into 6cm squares (or rounds) while still warm and pliable, then leave to cool completely. The tuiles will become crisp and brittle as they set. (If you find the tuile sheet is difficult to cut because it has cooled too much, return it to the oven for a minute to warm slightly.) Repeat with the remaining mixture. If not using immediately, store the polenta tuiles between layers of baking parchment in an airtight container.

# poached pears with sablé
## and blackberry sorbet {Serves 4}

2 poached pears (page 210)

**BLACKBERRY SORBET:**
150g caster sugar
30g liquid glucose
300ml water
juice of ½ lemon
550g ripe blackberries

**SABLÉ:**
30g icing sugar, plus extra to dust
125g unsalted butter, well softened
  but not melted
¼ split vanilla pod, seeds scraped
125g plain flour, sifted

**TO SERVE:**
4 polenta tuiles (page 211), optional | caramel cream (page 240) | vanilla pods (optional)

For the sorbet, put the sugar, liquid glucose and water in a saucepan and stir over a low heat to dissolve the sugar. Simmer for a few minutes to allow the syrup to thicken slightly, then take off the heat. Leave to cool completely, then add the lemon juice.

Whiz the berries and half the lemon sugar syrup in a blender or food processor to a purée. Push through a fine sieve into a bowl and mix with the rest of the sugar syrup. Pour into an ice-cream machine and churn until almost firm. Transfer to a suitable container and freeze overnight or until firm. (You'll have some extra sorbet for another dessert.)

For the sablé, sift the icing sugar into a bowl and mix in the softened butter, followed by the vanilla seeds. Mix well, but try not to aerate the mixture. Now incorporate the flour. The mixture may seem too dry to combine to begin with, but keep pushing the butter mix against the flour with a wooden spoon and it will eventually come together to form a dough. Roll out on a double layer of cling film, to form a log. Wrap the log in the cling film and roll on the work surface to even out the thickness. Chill for 1–2 hours until firm.

Preheat the oven to 180°C/Gas 4. Line 1 or 2 large baking sheets with a silicone liner. Unwrap the sablé log and slice thinly, using a sharp knife, into rounds about 5mm thick. Place, slightly apart, on the lined baking sheets and bake for 12–14 minutes until lightly golden around the edges. Remove and allow to cool and firm up. Dust with icing sugar before serving. (You'll only need 4 sablés for this dessert; store the rest in an airtight tin.)

To serve, halve the poached pears and scoop out the cores. Place each pear half on a serving plate. Top with a polenta tuile if using, followed by a neat quenelle of blackberry sorbet. Rest a sablé on the side of the pear and place a quenelle of caramel cream alongside. Add vanilla pods as a decoration to finish, if you like. Serve at once.

THE BEST PEARS *to use for this dessert are Williams, as these have a good deep flavour and poach perfectly, even if they slightly under-ripe. The sablé are the most amazing dessert biscuits I've ever made. They are fragile, but well worth the effort.*

# pear and star anise bread and butter pudding {Serves 4}

250ml double cream
250ml whole milk
2 star anise
3 large eggs
125g caster sugar
pinch of fine sea salt
30g butter, softened to room temperature
1 brioche loaf, thickly sliced
3–4 poached pears (page 210)
reduced sugar syrup (page 240), to glaze (optional)

Put the cream, milk and star anise into a saucepan and bring to the boil. Immediately turn off the heat and set aside to infuse and cool completely. Whisk the eggs and sugar together in a large bowl, then add the salt. Gradually pour in the cream and milk and whisk until smooth. Leave the star anise in the mixture, cover the bowl with cling film and chill overnight to allow the flavours to infuse.

The next day, strain the mixture through a fine sieve into a heavy-based saucepan. Stir over a low heat with a wooden spoon until it thickens to a light custard that is thick enough to lightly coat the back of the spoon. Strain the custard once again and set aside to cool.

Preheat the oven to 170°C/Gas 3. Lightly butter the brioche slices. Halve and core the poached pears, then cut into thin slices. Arrange the buttered brioche and pear slices in one large or four individual ovenproof dishes. Pour over the custard to cover and leave to stand for 20 minutes, to allow the brioche to soak up the custard. Top up with a little more custard if necessary.

Stand the dish(es) in one or two deep baking trays and pour in enough hot water to come halfway up the sides. Bake for 30–40 minutes for a large dish, or 20–25 minutes if using individual dishes, until the custards have set.

Remove from the oven and brush the surface generously with reduced sugar syrup to glaze, if you like. Let the pudding(s) stand for 5–10 minutes. Serve warm.

warm vanilla
rice pudding with
raspberries and thyme

chilled rice pudding
with cherry soup

champagne and
raspberry gratin

# warm vanilla rice pudding
## with raspberries and thyme {Serves 4–6}

500g whole milk
500g double cream
135g caster sugar

180g pudding rice
1 vanilla pod, split and seeds scraped
2 large egg yolks

**TO SERVE:**

crushed pecan ice cream (opposite) | raspberry and thyme jam (opposite) | few raspberries
few thyme leaves | 2–3 tbsp double cream (optional)

Put the milk, cream and 90g of the sugar into a heavy-based pan and stir over a low heat until the sugar has dissolved. Bring to the boil and immediately reduce the heat to a simmer. Tip in the rice and vanilla seeds and pod. Simmer very slowly for 45 minutes to 1 hour until the rice is tender, or cooked to your liking. Give the mixture a stir every once in a while to prevent the rice from catching and burning on the bottom of the pan.

Take the pan off the heat and remove the vanilla pod, then cover the surface with cling film and leave to stand for 15–20 minutes. The cling film will help prevent a skin from forming on top of the pudding.

Meanwhile, put the egg yolks and remaining 45g sugar in a heatproof bowl and set over a pan of barely simmering water. Using a hand-held electric whisk, beat the mixture until it is pale and thickened. Fold this through the rice pudding.

If serving warm, immediately spoon into warm bowls and serve little bowls of crushed pecan ice cream and raspberry jam topped with raspberries and thyme leaves on the side. If serving cold, allow to cool completely, then stir in a little cream to loosen the pudding before serving. (Any leftovers can be saved for chilled rice puddings with cherry soup, page 221).

THIS DESSERT *is one of my favourites. I developed a hatred for rice pudding during my schooldays, but this version has totally changed my view. You have to try it to believe how rich and delicious it is.*

# raspberry and thyme jam {Makes about 200g}

500g raspberries
80g caster sugar
1 thyme sprig, leaves only
2 tsp pectin

Put all the ingredients into a saucepan and slowly bring to the boil, stirring continuously to begin with to dissolve the sugar. Leave to simmer, stirring occasionally, for 8–10 minutes until any juices released from the raspberries have evaporated and the raspberry mixture has taken on a jammy consistency. To test if the jam is ready, check the temperature with a sugar thermometer: it should register 104°C. Alternatively, spoon a little jam onto a cold plate and chill for 5–10 minutes: the jam is ready if it sets and wrinkles when pushed with a finger.

While still warm, push the jam through a fine sieve into a bowl and discard the seeds and thyme leaves. Leave to cool completely, cover the bowl with cling film and chill until ready to use.

# crushed pecan ice cream {Makes about 800g}

40g caster sugar
20g water
100g pecans, lightly roasted
1 quantity partially churned vanilla ice cream (page 241)

Put the sugar and water into a saucepan and stir over a low heat until the sugar has dissolved, then increase the heat. Bring to the boil and boil rapidly until the syrup has thickened but not caramelised. Tip in the pecans and take the pan off the heat. Give the mixture a stir until the pecans are evenly coated with the sugar, then tip onto a silicone lined tray (or a lightly oiled tray). Leave to cool and set. The sugar will crystallise and become white and opaque as it cools.

Tip the sugared pecans into a large bowl and lightly crush with the tip of a rolling pin. Stir into the vanilla ice cream when it is almost frozen but not solid. Churn until the mixture is firm. Transfer to a freezerproof container and freeze for a few hours or overnight until set.

# chilled rice pudding
## with cherry soup {Serves 2-3}

50ml double cream, lightly whipped
½ quantity rice pudding (page 218)

**CHERRY SOUP:**
250g ripe cherries, stoned and roughly chopped
100ml sugar syrup (page 240)
25ml kirsch

**TO SERVE:**
polenta tuile rounds (page 211), optional │ 1 or 2 handfuls of ripe cherries

Line 2 or 3 pannacotta moulds or 6cm pastry rings with cling film and place on a baking tray. Fold the whipped cream into the rice pudding, then divide between the prepared moulds. Cover the moulds with cling film and chill for a few hours or overnight until set.

To make the cherry soup, put the cherries and sugar syrup into a saucepan and simmer for 4–6 minutes until the cherries are soft. Tip the cherries and syrup into a blender, add the kirsch and blitz to a very fine purée. Push the purée through a sieve into a bowl. Cool completely, then cover the bowl with cling film and chill.

When ready to serve, unmould the puddings by inverting into chilled bowls and peeling off the cling film, then lifting off the moulds. If using polenta tuiles, lay one on top of each rice pudding. Pour the cherry soup around each pudding and add a few cherries to each bowl. Serve at once.

COLD RICE PUDDING *may not sound inviting but, believe me, it is delicious with fruit. Cherries work really well, but you can use other fruit depending on the season. Try plums spiced with a little star anise, peaches infused with thyme, or apples scented with cinnamon.*

# champagne and raspberry gratin {Serves 4}

450g raspberries
55g caster sugar
2 large egg yolks
125ml double cream, lightly whipped
2–3 tbsp Champagne, to taste

**TO SERVE:**
handful of tiny mint leaves

Preheat the grill to its highest setting. Set aside about 20 of the largest raspberries for serving. Divide the rest between four individual ovenproof dishes and place the dishes on a large baking tray.

Put the sugar and egg yolks into a large heatproof bowl and set the bowl over a pan of barely simmering water. Using a hand-held electric whisk, beat the mixture until it is thick, creamy and tripled in volume. It should be thick enough to leave a ribbon trail on the surface when you lift the beaters. Fold in the cream and Champagne to taste.

Spoon the mixture over the raspberries and place the baking tray under the grill for about 3 minutes until the topping is golden and lightly caramelised. Remove and arrange the fresh raspberries on the side of the gratin. Scatter over the mint leaves and serve.

THIS IS *a very easy dessert that can be prepared in minutes. If you have a cook's blowtorch, you can simply wave it over the surface to caramelise the cream rather than pop it under the grill. And you can vary the soft fruit … try using sliced peaches, strawberries or blueberries, or a combination.*

chocolate moelleux
with milk and honey
ice cream and
pistachio sabayon

praline-coated
milk and honey
ice cream with
strawberry soup

individual
chocolate soufflés

# chocolate moelleux with milk and honey ice cream and pistachio sabayon

{Serves 8}

softened butter, to grease
cocoa powder, sifted, to coat
55g dark chocolate (about 70% cocoa solids), chopped
55g dark, bitter chocolate (about 85% cocoa solids), chopped
110g unsalted butter, diced
4 large eggs
3 large egg yolks
50g plain flour, sifted
150g caster sugar

**TO SERVE:**

melted chocolate, to decorate | crushed toasted pistachios, to sprinkle
chocolate paper (optional) | edible silver leaf (optional) | pistachio sabayon (opposite)
milk and honey ice cream (opposite) | caramel syrup, to drizzle (page 240), optional

You will need 8 small square metal moulds or ramekins, about 125ml capacity. Preheat the oven to 180°C/Gas 4. If using ramekins, line the bases with baking parchment. Brush the moulds well with butter, using upward strokes around the sides. Chill until firm, then repeat. Dust with cocoa powder, shaking out the excess. Set the moulds on a baking tray.

Melt all the chocolate and butter in a heatproof bowl set over a pan of simmering water. Stir until smooth. Take off the heat and allow to cool until tepid. Beat the eggs and yolks together, using an electric mixer, until pale and light. Mix the flour with the sugar, then fold into the whisked eggs. Finally, fold in the melted chocolate and butter mix.

Spoon the mixture into the moulds to three-quarters fill them. Bake for about 8–10 minutes until the chocolate moelleux is set around the edges but still moist and runny in the centre. The surface should look set but have a slight wobble. Let cool for a minute.

To assemble, you'll need to work quickly. If you like, decorate the serving plates with melted chocolate and crushed pistachios. Carefully run a small knife around the edges of each mould and invert onto the plates. Top the chocolate moelleux with chocolate paper squares and edible silver leaf, if using. (Or drizzle with melted chocolate and sprinkle with pistachios.) Spoon a little pistachio sabayon alongside. Place a scoop of milk and honey ice cream on the plate and drizzle over a little caramel syrup, if you like. Serve at once.

# pistachio sabayon {Makes about 400ml}

3 large egg yolks
125ml sugar syrup (page 240)
100g pistachio paste (ideally ready-made),
    otherwise homemade, page 242)
75ml whipping cream, softly whipped
a little extra whipping cream (optional)

Gently whisk the egg yolks in a large heatproof bowl using a hand-held electric whisk. Boil the sugar syrup in a heavy-based saucepan until it registers 118°C on a sugar thermometer. Immediately and slowly pour onto the egg yolks, whisking continuously. Keep whisking until the sides of the bowl no longer feel warm. Fold in the pistachio paste, followed by the whipped cream. For a thinner consistency, incorporate a little more cream.

# milk and honey ice cream {Makes about 1 litre}

1.25 litres whole milk
125ml double cream
15g liquid glucose
15g honey
145g condensed milk

Simmer the milk in a wide pan until reduced by half, regulating the heat so that it doesn't boil over. Leave to cool completely, then strain into a large bowl and mix together with all the other ingredients. Strain the mixture once again into an ice-cream machine. Churn until almost frozen. Transfer to a shallow freezerproof container and freeze until firm.

# chocolate paper {Makes about 32 squares (but allow for breakages}

Heat the oven to 180°C/Gas 4. Put 160g crème pâtissière (page 242) and 1 heaped tsp cocoa powder into a food processor and whiz until smooth. Pass through a fine sieve, then spread thinly on a silicone lined baking sheet with a palette knife. Use the tip of the knife to mark 8cm squares. Bake for 7–8 minutes until the 'chocolate paper' is set and no longer looks wet. Leave to cool for a minute. While still warm and pliable, run a small thin knife under each square and lift it off the liner. If you find that the chocolate paper is brittle and breaks as you try to lift it, return to a warm oven for another minute or two to soften slightly. When cooled, store in an airtight container between sheets of baking parchment.

# praline-coated milk and honey
# ice cream with strawberry soup {Serves 4}

**PRALINE:**

100g sugar

25g toasted flaked almonds

**STRAWBERRY SOUP:**

250g very ripe strawberries, hulled

2–3 tbsp icing sugar or sugar syrup (page 240)

**TO SERVE:**

milk and honey ice cream (page 227) | frozen hulled strawberries (preferably wild)

For the praline, line a baking tray with a silicone liner. Put the sugar into a wide pan and place over a high heat to melt and caramelise the sugar. When it has reached a rich caramel colour, remove the pan from the heat and tip in the flaked almonds. Pour the mixture onto the lined tray and spread it out with a spatula. Leave to cool completely until it is hard and brittle.

Break the praline into smaller pieces and put into a food processor, making sure it is perfectly dry. Blitz to fine crumbs, then tip out and store in an airtight container until ready to use.

To make the strawberry soup, put the strawberries into a blender or food processor and whiz to a fine purée. Taste and add a little icing sugar or sugar syrup to sweeten, if necessary. Pass the purée through a fine sieve into a bowl or jug and discard the seeds. Cover and chill for at least an hour.

When ready to serve, scoop the ice cream into neat round balls and roll them in the praline to coat. Place each ball in a chilled glass serving dish and decorate with the frozen strawberries. Pour the strawberry soup around the ice cream and serve at once.

# individual chocolate soufflés

{Serves 6}

softened butter, to grease
60g caster sugar, plus an extra 2–3 tbsp to dust
175g bitter chocolate (about 70% cocoa solids), chopped
4 large eggs, separated
drop of lemon juice
icing sugar, to dust

Preheat the oven to 200°C/Gas 6. You will need 6 small ramekins or little ovenproof basins, about 125ml capacity. Brush well with butter, using upward strokes around the sides. Chill until firm, then brush again with another layer of butter. Coat the ramekins with a little caster sugar, shaking out the excess. Place on a baking tray and set aside.

Put the chocolate into a heatproof bowl and set over a pan of barely simmering water. Stir a few times until the chocolate has melted and is smooth. Remove the bowl from the pan and leave to cool.

Whisk the egg whites in a large bowl until they form firm peaks. Add a drop of lemon juice and whisk in half of the caster sugar, a tablespoonful at a time, until the mixture forms stiff peaks.

Put the remaining caster sugar and egg yolks in a large heatproof bowl and whisk lightly. Set the bowl over the pan of barely simmering water and whisk until the mixture is light, glossy and has tripled in volume. Remove the bowl from the pan and whisk until the side of the bowl no longer feels warm.

Fold the egg yolk mixture into the cooled chocolate, then fold in a spoonful of the whisked egg whites, to loosen the mixture. Carefully fold in the rest of the egg whites until evenly combined. Spoon the mixture into the prepared ramekins and tap them lightly on the work surface to remove any large air pockets. Bake in the hot oven for 8–9 minutes or until the soufflés are well risen and just set on top. Dust with a little icing sugar and serve straightaway.

DARK, RICH CHOCOLATE
MOUSSES *can be made using the
same recipe. Simply divide the
soufflé mixture between individual
serving bowls and chill for a few
hours. Sprinkle generously with
grated chocolate to serve.*

maze cocktails

# maze cocktails

## cider 'n' black  {Serves 1}

Illustrated on page 232 (far left)

4 blackberries
10ml gomme syrup (or sugar syrup, page 240)
40ml vodka
10ml blackberry liqueur
10ml lime juice
30ml apple juice
cider, to top up
apple slice, to finish

Muddle (or crush) 3 blackberries with the gomme syrup in a cocktail shaker. Add the vodka, liqueur, lime juice and apple juice and shake well. Pour into a large cocktail glass filled with rock ice and top up with cider. Finish with an apple slice and a blackberry.

## crème brûlée  {Serves 1}

Illustrated on page 232 (second from left)

40ml Cognac
10ml amaretto di Saronno liqueur
10ml caramel liqueur
20ml double cream
chocolate sprinkles, to finish

Shake the spirit and liqueurs in a cocktail shaker, then strain into a well chilled Martini glass. Use the same shaker to shake the cream and float on the top of the drink. Finish with chocolate sprinkles.

# maze revolution    {Serves 1}

Illustrated on page 232 (third from left)

1 slice of pineapple, chopped
few raspberries
40ml Havana esp (golden rum)
15ml raspberry liqueur
20ml pineapple juice
10ml lime juice
10ml pomegranate juice
2 dashes of Peychaud bitters (optional)

Muddle (or crush) the pineapple and raspberries in a cocktail shaker, then add all the rest of the ingredients and shake well. Strain into a flute.

# fig sour    {Serves 1}

Illustrated on page 232 (fourth from left)

40ml vanilla-infused vodka
20ml lemon juice
10ml lime juice
10ml fig liqueur
10ml fig purée
5ml vanilla liqueur
1 small egg white
fig slice (optional)
lemon twist, to finish

Shake all the ingredients in a cocktail shaker and strain into a rocks glass filled with rock ice. Top with a fig slice if you like, and finish with a twist of lemon.

# arbuz {Serves 1}

Illustrated opposite

piece of watermelon, skinned and deseeded
½ lemongrass stalk
40ml vodka Zubrowka
10ml Citronge (Mexican orange liqueur)
5ml apple juice
5ml gomme syrup (or sugar syrup, page 240)
chunk of watermelon threaded with a piece of lemongrass,
    to finish

Muddle (or crush) the watermelon and lemongrass in
a cocktail shaker, then add the rest of the ingredients.
Shake vigorously and strain into a well chilled Martini
glass. Garnish with the watermelon and lemongrass.


# jason's bloody mary {Serves 1}

Illustrated on page 233 (far right)

50ml chilli-infused vodka
50ml tomato juice
5ml orange juice
pinch of celery salt
pinch of black pepper
½ tsp horseradish cream
a couple of drops of Worcestershire sauce
piece of celery, to finish

Shake all the ingredients in a cocktail shaker and strain
into a large cocktail glass filled with rock ice. Garnish
with a piece of celery.

# basics

# sugar syrup {Makes about 750ml}

500g caster sugar
500ml water
squeeze of lemon juice (optional)

Put the sugar and water in a saucepan over a low heat to dissolve the sugar. Increase the heat and bring to the boil. Let bubble for a few minutes to thicken slightly, then take off the heat and add the lemon juice if required. Cool and chill if not using immediately.

**LIGHT SUGAR SYRUP:** Reduce the sugar quantity by half.

**REDUCED SUGAR SYRUP:** If a recipe calls for reduced sugar syrup, simply boil the syrup until reduced by about half until thickened and syrupy.

# vanilla sugar syrup

{Makes about 250ml}

100g caster sugar
200ml water
1 vanilla pod

Put the sugar and water in a small saucepan over a low heat. When the sugar has dissolved, increase the heat and bring to the boil. Split the vanilla pod lengthways, scrape out the seeds and add them to the sugar syrup along with the empty pod. Take off the heat and leave the syrup to infuse as it cools. Remove the pod from the sugar syrup before using.

# caramel syrup {Makes 160g}

125g caster sugar
55ml hot water
½ tsp black treacle

Put the sugar into a heavy-based saucepan over a medium-high heat and allow to dissolve and caramelise, without moving the pan. When it has reached a rich caramel colour, take the pan off the heat. Protecting your hand with an oven glove, carefully pour in the hot water and stand back as the caramel will spit and splutter viciously. Return the pan to a low heat and stir until any lumps of caramel have dissolved and the syrup is smooth. Stir in the black treacle, simmer for 5 minutes and remove from the heat. Leave to cool completely.

# caramel cream {Makes 250ml}

50ml double cream
150ml whipping cream
40g caramel syrup (above)
½ tsp icing sugar
½ tsp brandy

Put the creams, caramel syrup and icing sugar into a large bowl and whisk to firm peaks. Fold through the brandy. Shape into neat quenelles to serve.

# vanilla crème anglaise

{Makes about 300ml}

125ml double cream
125ml whole milk
1 vanilla pod
35g caster sugar
3 large egg yolks

Put the cream and milk into a heavy-based saucepan. Split the vanilla pod lengthways and scrape out the seeds with the back of the knife. Add these to the pan along with the empty pod and heat slowly until it is almost starting to boil. Take off the heat and set aside to let the vanilla infuse the creamy milk as it cools.

Beat the sugar and egg yolks together in a large bowl until smooth and creamy. When cooled, pour the vanilla cream onto the egg mix, whisking to combine, then pour this mixture through a fine sieve into the cleaned saucepan.

Stir continuously over a low heat, using a wooden spoon, until thickened to a light custard, which is thick enough to lightly coat the back of the spoon. Immediately pour into a bowl.

If you're not using the custard straight away, cool it down quickly by setting the bowl in a larger bowl of iced water. Stir occasionally to prevent a skin from forming. Chill and use within a few days.

# vanilla ice cream

{Makes about 700g}

250ml double cream
250ml whole milk
2 vanilla pods
100g caster sugar
6 large egg yolks

Pour the double cream and milk into a heavy-based saucepan. Split the vanilla pods lengthways and scrape out the seeds with the back of a knife. Add both the seeds and pods to the pan and slowly bring to the boil.

Meanwhile, beat the sugar and egg yolks together in a bowl. As soon as the creamy milk bubbles up the side of the pan, remove from the heat and slowly trickle the liquid onto the sugary yolks, beating well. When fully incorporated, pour the mixture back into the cleaned pan and stir over a medium-low heat with a wooden spoon until the mixture thickens enough to thinly coat the back of the spoon. Leave to cool completely, then pass through a sieve into a bowl.

Pour the mixture into an ice-cream machine and churn until smooth and thick. Transfer to a freezerproof container and freeze until needed.

## crème pâtissière {Makes about 550ml}

300ml whole milk
200ml double cream
1 vanilla pod
4 large egg yolks
75g caster sugar
40g cornflour

Pour the milk and cream into a heavy-based saucepan. Split the vanilla pod lengthways and scrape out the seeds with the back of the knife. Add these to the pan along with the empty vanilla pod and slowly bring to the boil.

Meanwhile, beat the egg yolks and sugar together in a bowl, then mix in the cornflour until smooth. As soon as the creamy milk comes to the boil, take the pan off the heat and slowly pour the liquid onto the egg yolk mixture, whisking continuously. Strain the mixture through a fine sieve into the cleaned pan. Stir over a low heat until the mixture is smooth and thick, then increase the heat and simmer, stirring, for 4–5 minutes to cook out the cornflour.

Pour into a bowl and cover the surface with cling film to prevent a skin forming. Leave to cool completely, then chill if not using immediately.

## pistachio paste {Makes about 200g}

150ml sugar syrup (page 240)
100g roasted and skinned pistachios

Bring the sugar syrup to the boil in a saucepan, then immediately tip in the pistachios and stir to mix. Transfer to a blender or a food processor and blitz to a very fine paste, then push through a fine sieve into a bowl.

The pistachio paste can be kept chilled for up to 2 days if not using immediately. You'll need to bring it back to room temperature before using, as it is thick and difficult to incorporate when chilled.

## clarified butter
{Makes about 200g}

250g unsalted butter

Put the butter into a saucepan and heat slowly, giving it a stir from time to time. Once melted, the butter will separate and the milk solids will float to the surface as a foam. Take the pan off the heat. Using a wide spoon, skim off the milk solids. Pour the golden fat through a muslin-lined sieve into a jug.

If properly chilled, the clarified butter will keep well for a couple of months.

# chicken stock {Makes about 1.5-2 litres}

1.5kg chicken bones
about 3 litres cold water
1½ celery sticks, trimmed and roughly
  chopped
1 leek (white part only), trimmed and roughly
  chopped
2 onions, peeled and roughly chopped
¼ garlic bulb, unpeeled
1 thyme sprig

Put the chicken bones into a large stockpot and pour in just enough cold water to cover. Bring to the boil and skim off the scum that rises to the surface, then turn the heat down as low as possible. Add all the remaining ingredients, making sure they are all fully submerged in the water. Let the stock simmer for 3–4 hours then pass it through a muslin-lined sieve into a bowl. Allow to cool.

If not using the stock immediately, refrigerate and use within 5 days, or divide into convenient quantities and freeze in suitable containers.

# veal stock {Makes about 1.5-2 litres}

1.5kg veal or beef bones
75ml olive oil
1 large onion, peeled and roughly chopped
2 large carrot, peeled and roughly chopped
2 celery sticks, peeled and roughly chopped
¼ garlic bulb, unpeeled
1½ tbsp tomato purée
5 litres cold water
1 thyme sprig
1 bay leaf

Preheat the oven to 220°C/Gas 7. Put the veal bones in a roasting tin, drizzle with half the olive oil and roast in the oven for about 1 hour until golden brown. Heat the remaining oil in a large stockpot and add the chopped vegetables and garlic. Stir frequently over a medium heat until the vegetables are lightly golden. Add the tomato purée and stir for another 2–3 minutes.

Add the browned veal bones to the stockpot, leaving behind the excess fat. Pour over the cold water to cover and bring to a gentle simmer. Skim off any scum that rises to the surface. Add the herbs and let simmer for 5–6 hours. Strain the stock through a muslin-lined sieve into a clean pan. Return to the heat and boil until reduced by half.

If not using immediately, allow to cool and freeze in batches, or refrigerate and use within 5 days.

# fish stock {Makes about 1.5 litres}

1.5kg white fish bones (such as turbot, brill, halibut), washed
2 tbsp olive oil
1 onion, peeled and roughly chopped
1 leek (white part only), trimmed and roughly chopped
1 celery stick, trimmed and roughly chopped
1 small fennel bulb, roughly chopped
3 garlic cloves, peeled
300ml white wine
1 bay leaf
1 thyme sprig
few parsley stalks
10 white peppercorns
1 lemon, sliced
2 litres cold water

Chop the fish bones into smaller pieces and set aside. Heat the olive oil in a large pan and sweat the onion, leek, celery, fennel and garlic for 4–5 minutes. Pour in the white wine and let bubble until reduced to a syrupy glaze. Add the herbs, peppercorns, lemon slices and fish bones to the pot. Cover with the water and bring to a simmer, skimming off the scum that rise to the surface. Gently simmer for 20 minutes.

Let the stock cool and settle, then strain it through a muslin-lined sieve. Freeze in smaller quantities if not using at once, or refrigerate and use within 2 or 3 days.

# vegetable stock {Makes about 1.5 litres}

5 carrots, trimmed and roughly chopped
2 onions, trimmed and roughly chopped
2 celery sticks, trimmed and roughly chopped
1 leek (white part only), trimmed and roughly chopped
1.5–2 litres cold water
few basil sprigs
few chervil sprigs
few chives
½ garlic bulb
2 star anise
6 coriander seeds
6 white peppercorns
6 pink peppercorns
200ml dry white wine
1 lemon, cut into wedges

Put the vegetables into a stockpot, cover with the cold water and bring to the boil. Lower the heat and simmer for about 10 minutes. Add all the remaining ingredients to the pot, ensuring that they are fully submerged in the water. Simmer for a further 2 minutes, then add the white wine and lemon wedges. Turn off the heat and leave to cool completely.

Chill for 24 hours, dividing the stock into smaller batches if the stockpot does not fit into your fridge.

The following day, pass the stock through a muslin-lined sieve. Freeze in smaller portions if not using straightaway, or refrigerate and use within 5 days.

# red wine sauce {Makes about 250ml}

2 tbsp olive oil
beef trimmings (optional)
2 shallots, peeled and finely chopped
1 garlic clove, peeled and chopped
few thyme sprigs
1 bay leaf
splash of sherry vinegar
1 glass of port
750ml bottle of red wine
6 peppercorns
500ml chicken stock (page 243)
500ml veal stock (page 243)
sea salt and black pepper

Heat the olive oil in a pan, add the beef trimmings if using, and fry until browned. Add the shallots with the garlic, thyme and bay leaf and cook over a medium heat, stirring occasionally, for 5–6 minutes until soft. Add the sherry vinegar, stirring to deglaze, then pour in the port and red wine. Bring to the boil and let bubble briskly until reduced down to a sticky glaze. Add the peppercorns and pour in the stocks. Bring to a simmer and cook for 20 minutes, skimming off any scum that rises to the surface occasionally.

Pass the sauce through a muslin-lined sieve into a clean pan. Return to the heat and simmer until reduced to a rich sauce consistency. Season with salt and pepper to taste.

# madeira sauce {Makes about 250ml}

2 tbsp olive oil
2 shallots, peeled and sliced
2 garlic cloves, peeled and roughly chopped
1 bay leaf
5 thyme sprigs
¼ tsp black peppercorns
100ml white wine
100ml Madeira
20ml honey
150ml chicken stock (page 243)
150ml veal stock (page 243)
sea salt and black pepper

Heat the olive oil in a saucepan and sauté the shallots with the garlic, bay leaf, thyme and peppercorns over a medium heat for 5–6 minutes until softened and golden brown.

Add the white wine and Madeira and let bubble until reduced down to a sticky glaze. Add the honey and cook for 2–3 minutes. Pour in the stocks and cook until reduced by two-thirds to a syrupy consistency.

Strain through a fine sieve into a clean pan. Reheat, if necessary, and season with salt and pepper to taste.

# tomato fondue {Makes about 215g}

500g vine-ripened tomatoes
2 tbsp olive oil
3 shallots, peeled and finely chopped
1 garlic clove, peeled and finely chopped
1 thyme sprig
1 bay leaf
1 tbsp tomato purée
1–2 tbsp vinaigrette (page 246)
sea salt and black pepper
pinch of caster sugar (optional)

Bring a pan of water to the boil, then take off the heat. Lightly score the top and base of the tomatoes with a sharp knife. Immerse them in the hot water for a minute, then drain and refresh under cold running water. Peel off the skins, then cut the tomatoes into quarters and remove the seeds. Finely chop the flesh.

Heat the olive oil in a pan and add the shallots, garlic, thyme and bay leaf. Sauté for 3–4 minutes until the shallots begin to soften, then stir in the tomato purée and sauté for another 2 minutes. Tip in the tomatoes and cook over a medium-high heat for 10–12 minutes until the tomato juices have cooked off and the pan is quite dry. Stir in the vinaigrette, then season with salt, pepper and a pinch of sugar to taste.

For a smooth sauce, pass the mixture through a fine sieve. Allow to cool, then store in a sealed jar in the fridge and use within 4–5 days.

# mayonnaise {Makes about 300ml}

2 large egg yolks
1 tsp Dijon mustard
sea salt and black pepper
275ml pomace oil (or light olive oil)
2 tsp white wine vinegar

Put the egg yolks, mustard and a little seasoning into a small food processor and whiz until thick and smooth. With the motor running, very slowly trickle in the oil. The mixture should be thick and creamy. Add the wine vinegar, then adjust the seasoning. For a lighter consistency, thin the mayonnaise down with 1–2 tbsp warm water. Transfer to a bowl or jar, cover and refrigerate. Use within 3 days.

**NOTE:** If the mixture curdles as you are adding the oil, transfer it to a jug and add another egg yolk to the food processor bowl. Start again, by blending the curdled mixture slowly into the egg yolk, and the mayonnaise should re-emulsify.

# vinaigrette {Makes 350ml}

50ml white wine vinegar
300ml extra-virgin olive oil
sea salt and black pepper

Put all the ingredients into a jug and blitz, using a hand-held stick blender, to emulsify. Alternately, shake in a screw-topped jar. Store in the fridge for up to a week and shake well before each use.

# tartare sauce {Makes about 250ml}

200ml mayonnaise
10 cornichons or 1 large gherkin, finely diced
2 tbsp capers, chopped
1 shallot, peeled and finely diced
1 tbsp chopped parsley
sea salt and black pepper
squeeze of lemon juice

Combine all the ingredients in a bowl and stir until evenly blended, seasoning with salt, pepper and lemon juice to taste. Cover and refrigerate. Use within a day or two.

# tapenade {Makes about 270g}

200g pitted black olives
40g anchovy fillets in olive oil, drained
20g capers, rinsed and drained
1 garlic clove, peeled
1 tbsp olive oil, plus extra to drizzle

Blend all the ingredients together in a food processor until smooth. Spoon into a clean jar and cover with a thin layer of olive oil; this helps to preserve the tapenade. Chill and use within a week.

# shallot confit {Makes about 200g}

9 banana shallots, peeled
200ml olive oil
1 thyme sprig
sea salt

Finely dice the shallots. Place them in a heavy-based pan with the olive oil, thyme and a sprinkling of salt. Cook over a very low heat for 30 minutes or until the shallots are translucent and very soft. Allow to cool, then discard the thyme.

Store the confit in an airtight container in a cool place and use as required, within a week. Drain off excess oil before using.

# garlic confit {Makes about 100g}

2 garlic bulbs
250ml olive oil
pinch of sea salt

Separate and peel the garlic cloves, then put them in a small saucepan and pour over the olive oil to cover. Add a sprinkling of salt. Lay a piece of crumpled greaseproof paper over the surface and place the pan over a very low heat. Cook gently for 30–45 minutes until the garlic is very soft.

If not using immediately, store in a clean jar, making sure that the garlic is submerged in the olive oil. Keep in a cool place and use within a week. Drain off excess oil before using.

# garlic potatoes {Serves 6}

1.5kg large Charlotte potatoes
1 garlic bulb, split horizontally
small bunch of thyme
sea salt and black pepper
1.5–2 litres melted duck fat (or olive oil)
30g butter, chopped
6 coriander seeds, lightly crushed
2 tbsp chopped coriander leaves

Wash and dry the potatoes well. Place them in a pan with one half of the split garlic bulb and the thyme. Add a little seasoning, then pour on the duck fat to cover. Simmer over a very low heat for about 20 minutes until slightly under-cooked; the potatoes should have a slight resistance when pierced with a small sharp knife. Remove from the pan with a slotted spoon and peel while still hot, protecting your hands with rubber gloves. Let cool completely, then slice into 5mm thick rounds.

When ready to serve, sauté the potato rounds in batches. Melt a few knobs of butter in a wide frying pan. Add the other garlic half and the coriander seeds and fry until the garlic is lightly golden on the cut side. Lay the potatoes in the foaming butter in a single layer. Season well and fry for 2½–3 minutes on each side until golden brown and tender. Drain on kitchen paper and keep warm, while you sauté the remaining potatoes. Scatter over the chopped coriander and serve.

# coriander carrots {Serves 6}

400g baby carrots
sea salt and black pepper
small bunch of coriander, stalks
    separated and leaves chopped
20g butter
6 coriander seeds, lightly crushed

Wash and trim the tops from the baby carrots. Bring a pan of salted water to the boil. Have ready a bowl of iced water. Add the baby carrots to the boiling water with the coriander stalks and blanch for 3–4 minutes until just tender. Drain and refresh in the iced water; drain again. Discard the coriander stalks.

A few minutes before you are ready to serve, melt the butter in a frying pan. Add the coriander seeds and the blanched carrots and toss over a high heat until the carrots are lightly caramelised. Season well with salt and pepper. Drain off the excess butter and toss with the chopped coriander leaves before serving.

# braised baby onions

{Serves 4-6}

1 tbsp olive oil
30g butter
20 baby pearl onions, peeled
1 tsp caster sugar
100–200ml chicken stock (page 243)

Heat a small pan, then add the olive oil and butter. Tip in the onions and fry for 4–5 minutes until golden brown all over. Add the sugar, toss well and cook for a few more minutes until the sugar has caramelised.

Carefully strain off the excess butter from the pan and add the chicken stock. Increase the heat and boil until the stock has reduced to a syrupy glaze. Pierce the onions with a metal skewer to check that they are tender. If not, add a little more stock to the pan and boil again until reduced to a glaze.

# braised baby fennel

{Serves 2-4}

1 ½ tbsp olive oil
4 baby fennel, trimmed
sea salt and black pepper
splash of vegetable stock (page 244) or water

Heat the olive oil in a pan and add the fennel with a little seasoning. Fry, turning, until golden brown, then add a splash of vegetable stock and cover the pan. Braise for 6–8 minutes until the fennel is tender when pierced with a small sharp knife. Drain before serving.

# fennel purée    {Serves 3-4}

1 large fennel, trimmed and chopped
150ml double cream
sea salt and black pepper

Put the fennel, cream and some seasoning in a small pan. Bring to a simmer, cover and cook for 8–10 minutes until the fennel is very soft. Transfer to a food processor and blend to a fine purée. Warm through in a pan over a low heat to serve.

# pickled ginger {Makes 200g}

125g fresh root ginger
125g caster sugar
60ml water
60ml white wine vinegar

Bring a pan of water to the boil. Have a bowl of iced water ready on the side. Peel and thinly slice the ginger, using a swivel vegetable peeler or mandolin. Blanch the ginger slices in the boiling water for a few seconds, then immediately transfer to the iced water, using a slotted spoon. Repeat the process once more. Drain well.

Put the sugar, water and wine vinegar into a saucepan and stir over a low heat until the sugar has dissolved. Bring to the boil, then reduce the heat to a simmer. Add the ginger slices and simmer for 30 minutes until they are tender, but still retaining a slight crunch.

# piccalilli {Makes about 1.6kg}

750g cauliflower, cut into florets
fine sea salt
550ml white wine vinegar
300ml malt vinegar
200g caster sugar
1 tbsp ground turmeric
30g English mustard powder
1½ tbsp cornflour, mixed with 2–3 tbsp water
300g silverskin onions
200g cornichons, drained and diced

Cut the cauliflower into small florets, spread out on a large tray and sprinkle with salt. Cover with cling film and leave in a cool place overnight.

The next day, rinse the cauliflower under cold running water and drain well.

Put the vinegars into a wide pan, bring to the boil and boil steadily for about 20 minutes until reduced by a quarter. Mix the sugar, turmeric and mustard together, then add to the pan and stir until the sugar has dissolved. Simmer for a few minutes. Stir in the cornflour mixture and cook, stirring, for another 4–5 minutes to cook out the cornflour.

Tip in the cauliflower and onions and stir well. Simmer for 2 minutes, then take off the heat and add the cornichons. Give the mixture a good stir. Spoon into sterilised jars and seal immediately. Try not to use metal-topped jars as the vinegar will rust the metal. The piccalilli is best left to mature for a few weeks before serving.

# cep brioche {Makes about 36 small brioche}

450g strong white bread flour, plus
    extra to dust
1 heaped tsp (about 7g) fine sea salt
20g caster sugar
15g fresh yeast (or 7g dried active yeast)
60ml tepid whole milk
4 large eggs, lightly beaten
200g unsalted butter, softened, plus
    extra to brush
10g dried ceps (or porcini)
about 120g cep purée (page 49)
1 large egg yolk, beaten with 1 tbsp
    milk, to glaze
coarse sea salt, to sprinkle
cep butter, to serve (page 49), optional

Sift the flour and salt into the bowl of a free-standing electric mixer fitted with a dough hook. Stir in the sugar and make a well in the centre. Dissolve the yeast in the milk in a small bowl, then add to the well along with the eggs and butter. Set the machine on low speed to combine the ingredients, mixing until the dough is soft and sticky. Increase the speed and mix until the dough comes together. It should be quite smooth and elastic. If it appears too wet, incorporate a little more flour.

Remove the bowl from the machine and cover with lightly oiled cling film. Leave the dough to prove slowly in the fridge for about 8 hours or overnight until it doubles in volume.

Grind the dried ceps in a small food processor or spice grinder to a fine powder. Store in an airtight container.

Divide the risen dough in two to make it easier to work with. Roll out one half on a lightly floured surface to a rectangle, about 1cm thick. Spread a layer of cep purée over the dough, leaving a 2cm border free around the edge, then dust the purée with cep powder. Roll up the dough into a long log, then place it on a lightly oiled baking sheet. Repeat the process with the remaining dough. Lightly cover the logs with a piece of lightly oiled cling film and place in the fridge for an hour.

Brush three 12-hole mini muffin tins or flexible silicone muffin moulds with butter and dust lightly with flour (or you can bake the brioche in three batches). Remove the dough from the fridge and slice into neat 25–30g pieces. Roll them lightly into round balls and set them in the prepared moulds. (If the dough gets too soft and greasy, return it to the fridge and chill until firm.) Lightly cover the dough with oiled cling film and leave to prove until risen over the top of the moulds to resemble little mushrooms. The brioche are ready to be baked when little indentations are left if you gently press them with a finger.

Preheat the oven to 190°C/Gas 5. Brush the tops of the dough with the egg wash. Bake for 12–15 minutes until the tops are brown. Remove from the oven and transfer to a wire rack to cool slightly. Serve them warm, sprinkled with a little coarse sea salt, and spread with some cep butter if you like.

# index

## acknowledgements

This book has been an ambition since I first started to cook. It has been a pleasure to do and I would like to thank all those who have worked so hard to make it really special: Anne Furniss for having the vision to commission me; Helen Lewis for being so creative and putting together a formidable team; Janet Illsley for editing the book and chasing me to finish on time; and Emily Quah for her tireless work testing all of the recipes in the home kitchen. Special thanks to Ditte Isager, who is one of the great food photographers in my opinion – these photos just blow me away; and to Lucy for the wonderful props.

I am particularly grateful to James Durrant for always being there, not only on this book but throughout the life of Maze. He is a talented chef – one you will hear more of in the future. Thanks also to Chris Whitmore who worked alongside James on my food and to all my kitchen staff, led by Paul Hood in London and Phil Carmichael in Prague. Last, but not least, thank you to Gordon and Chris for giving me the opportunity to shine in the restaurant world, which has been my lifelong dream.